Caro

Manifesting

✳

LOVE &
PROSPERITY

How to Attract the
Happiness you Deserve

GODSFIELD

An Hachette UK Company
www.hachette.co.uk

First published in Great Britain in 2023
by Godsfield, an imprint of
Octopus Publishing Group Ltd
Carmelite House
50 Victoria Embankment
London EC4Y 0DZ
www.octopusbooks.co.uk

ISBN 978-1-84181-544-2

A CIP catalogue record for this book is available from the British Library.

Printed and bound in UK

10 9 8 7 6 5 4 3 2 1

This FSC® label means that materials used for the product have been responsibly sourced

MIX
Paper from
responsible sources
FSC® C104740

Publisher: Lucy Pessell
Senior Editor: Hannah Coughlin
Designer: Isobel Platt
Assistant Editor: Samina Rahman
Production Controller: Serena Savini
Illustration: p.43 Yoga Pose Chakras by Oleksandr Panasovskyi from Noun Project

This material was previously published as *The Spiritual Guide to Attracting Love*
and *The Spiritual Guide to Attracting Prosperity*

Contents

Introduction

'Great things are not done by impulse,
but by a series of small things
brought together'

Vincent Van Gogh

Would you like to be happier and more fulfilled than you are now? Have you ever wondered what it will take to find someone who really loves you? Do you want to be richer than you are now? Is it your greatest wish to be loved by someone who loves you as much as you love them?

Is it your dream to live a life where you can be yourself, perhaps surrounded by loving friends, partner and family?

Or do you wish to let go of money worries and create the freedom to do what you want to do with your life?

Most of us want to attract love and prosperity into our lives – they are two key foundations to human life. This book will show you how to manifest these things into your daily life, using methods that have worked for people throughout the ages. I will show you how to use the Law of Attraction and the wisdom of some of the most ancient spiritual traditions on the planet in order to attract love into your life, helping you to heal past wounds and to live a nurturing joyful life. I will show you how to attract prosperity into your life, and why 'prosperity' is different from 'money'. You can have a high income or lots of cash in the bank and still not be prosperous. You can also feel prosperous with little money when it is used in the right way.

Using simple but effective techniques and rituals, you will learn to empower yourself to manifest the changes you want in your life. You don't need to believe in a particular religion or faith – the ways of thinking and techniques are suitable whatever your background or culture. Even if you have already looked into manifestation, visualization, goal-setting or cosmic ordering, if you haven't yet got what you want, I believe this book can help.

The information here is taken from a wide range of ancient knowledge and wisdom from around the globe, the primary purpose of which is the following: to change your ways of being in your mind, body and spirit so that you can bring the love and prosperity you truly want into your life.

The aim of this book is to help you to create a permanent shift in your

Use the Law of Attraction and the wisdom of ancient spiritual traditions to attract love and prosperity into your life.

life. If you truly take this method on board, it will move you from a place where you lack hope and lack what you want, through to the birth of hope and expectation, and on to the realization of your goals.

What is Love?

Love has been baffling humans for thousands of years. What is it? It has been described in the past as a power with more force than a besieging army or a priceless commodity because it is the only thing you can give away and still keep. What does love mean for you?

We all have our own definitions of love. However, I think it is universally accepted that love is a basic human need. From the moment we leave the womb to the

> # It is universally accepted that love is a basic human need.

moment of death, we all share this need to feel love.

This book is focused primarily on romantic relationships, showing you how to attract a loving partner into your life. At the same time, love can come to us in many forms throughout our lives: in the form of loving platonic friendships, family love, the love of children, and of course love from a romantic partner.

The love-attraction formula

This book introduces ways in which you can bring love into your life. These fit into a basic method, which I call the Love-attraction Formula. When you follow this formula you can change your life and bring into it the love you desire in whatever form you want it.

✳ **Step 1, Believe:** Examine and, if necessary, change your beliefs. Sometimes changing your thoughts is a very simple process — recognizing what they are, identifying new beliefs and adopting them. Sometimes, if we have had particularly damaging life experiences, some healing of the past is required first.

✳ **Step 2, Become loving:** Treat yourself in exactly the way you wish others to treat you. When you love yourself and don't need other people to make you happy, you will paradoxically attract more people who want to make you happy and love you.

✳ **Step 3, Decide your future:** Identify what you really want to manifest in your life. If you have a vision that is possible, if not probable, to achieve, then as long as your beliefs support you, you will be able to achieve that vision.

✳ **Step 4, Build up energy:** By asking for help from the spiritual universe, the invisible world of energy around us, we attract energy to our dreams, rather like powering up a rechargeable battery.

What exactly is Prosperity?

Let's start with some introductions. Meet some people that I know:

Emma inherited a million at about thirty-five but has always lived a bit like a student: in an apartment with no mortgage, filled with second-hand furniture, working part-time and hanging out with friends. She does not feel financially well-off and worries that she might lose what she gained as easily as she came into it.

Ryan grew up in a middle-income family. He began investing and researching the property market early in life and ten years on, he owns five properties and earns a million a year. But he has had a disastrous love life – he spent so much time thinking about money that he never made the time to spend with his partner or his family.

Annette is married to a self-made millionaire. To many people she can do anything she likes without considering the cost. But she does not buy designer clothes or travel around in a flashy car; she is scared of not having money one day because she did not do any work to attract it in the first place.

Rebecca is a successful freelancer and commands unusually high fees for her services in the creative field. She earns a six-figure annual income but spends it quickly, always the first one to pay for drinks and going on exotic vacations. A year ago,

Rebecca went bankrupt when she was refused any more loans. She had never bought a home or any permanent asset. Right now, she is staying with friends, and she has destroyed her credit card.

Attitudes to money

Do you consider any of the people mentioned to be prosperous? Certainly, some of them have had access to huge amounts of money. Some of them have had it handed to them on a plate. Others took every opportunity they could find to make money whenever they were offered it. Personally, though, I would not call any of them particularly prosperous. Prosperity, I suggest, is a state of mind and the following rules apply:

* There is no point having money if you have a rotten life.

* There is no point having money if you get into debt and the stress causes you to become ill.

* There is no point living from pay cheque to pay cheque if it prevents you from having financial freedom to do what you love. In the end you will never feel fulfilled.

All these people I have introduced you to control their futures by the ways in which they think – as indeed do you and I. Money is simply a medium, a means you can use to create a particular way of living, not an end in itself. You alone are responsible for taking control of it and creating your own definition of a prosperous life by using wealth wisely, rather than letting it control you.

What do you think Emma, Ryan, Annette and Rebecca believe about money that has meant they have attracted the particular circumstances of their lives? Obviously only the individuals involved can answer that question precisely, but it is possible to imagine they have differing attitudes toward money and what these might be.

If you have grown up with negative attitudes toward money or you have a lack of financial literacy generally, you will keep attracting a lack of prosperity into your life. This will happen in one of three ways. You will not attract money at all. Or perhaps you will attract money but spend more than you earn and get into debt. Thirdly, you will attract money, but the very fact of having that money causes the rest of your life to fall apart. For example, you can spend so much time out earning that your relationship falls apart. Alternatively, when you have finally earned the money, you may have become so stressed by the having and the keeping of it that you fall ill.

What is your definition of prosperity?

Take some time to really think about what your definition of prosperity is. For me, having prosperity in my life means that I have enough money to do what I want at the same time as finding fulfilment in work and every other part of my life. Work out exactly what your definition is, deliberately and carefully, otherwise you may manifest bucket loads of money, but end up in a position similar to any of the people I have introduced above.

> ## Prosperity is the real means to living a happy and fulfilled life.

Knowing your definition of prosperity — and you will be asked to think about this in much more detail in subsequent chapters — is the key to creating change. You need to know the end goal of your journey to prosperity before you embark on that journey.

What is your attitude toward money now?

As well as knowing where you are heading, it is important to know the starting point of your journey to prosperity. Otherwise, how are you going to be able to know what needs changing in your current world? You can begin by thinking about your current attitudes toward money.

There are all sorts of people with many differing attitudes to money. Some familiar examples include those who:

* Earn a lot and save a lot, but do not enjoy themselves.
* Earn a little, save a lot and have a good time.
* Earn well, save well, and have a 'rich', full life.
* Earn little, spend lots and have fun now, but have nothing saved for the future.

What is your own mindset when it comes to wealth and what would you like it to be like instead?

As you continue reading, allow this question to remain in your mind. Do not worry if you do not have the answers to this or any other questions immediately – your mind will eventually come up with it if you keep your thoughts open and your mind receptive.

Creating wealth for the right reasons

This guide will also help you to create wealth, but it is only a worthwhile goal when used as a route to attracting real prosperity in your life. It is important to state from the outset that money should never be the end goal, only a means to what you want to achieve by having it. While you need money on a practical level in order to live your daily life, prosperity is the real means to living a happy and fulfilled life. It can be said that you are prosperous when you are able to live a life that makes you happy, meaning that you are happy because you are able to do what you want to do. This also implies your prosperity goes hand in hand with your spiritual wellbeing.

Of course, money is an important part of prosperity, and this book will show you how to create specific goals which, if they match yours, and work alongside and in conjunction with your overall life aspirations, will bring you happiness.

Manifesting for Prosperity

The prosperity section of this book is best read in chronological order because there is a natural step-by-step way of manifesting a life of abundance and prosperity. Once you understand the general method, you may want to go back to particular techniques and practise them again. Generally, it is a good idea to practise all the techniques more than once. Some rituals, for example those in step 4, are designed for consistent practice.

* Step 1, Check your thoughts: How the Law of Attraction affects your current levels of prosperity and how to develop maximum prosperity beliefs.

* Step 2, Find your flow: How feeling gratitude can make you into a natural prosperity attractor.

* Step 3, Decide your future: Vital steps to make a difference in turning your desired future into a reality, rather than something you 'want', with several powerful exercises to ensure you create prosperity, not just money.

* Step 4, Play your part: Learn that you and the universe are co-creators of your life.

* Step 5: Prosperity rituals: Age-old rituals and prosperity props to keep your energetic vibration boosted to its maximum level.

* Step 6: Your prosperity helpers: Choose a spiritual helper that you can turn to for support in your quest for prosperity.

* Step 7: Daydream your future: Creative visualization and active meditation techniques to boost your manifestation power by removing blocks and activating your dreams.

* Step 8: Living the Future: What to do next to make sure your dreams of prosperity really do become a reality.

What can you expect to change in your life?

How will you know when you have truly attracted lasting love into your life? And how prosperous can you expect to become by putting these principles into action?

You can expect your life to change to the degree that you believe it is possible to change. The results are entirely dependent on you. I personally believe that you can achieve extraordinary change. I would suggest that it would be helpful for you to believe this, too!

This is a universe of infinite possibilities. It really doesn't matter when you begin your journey, only which path you decide to take. If you make the changes, you will become the change in your own life.

Obviously, this book cannot promise that you will necessarily become the wealthiest person on the planet. Or immediately find true love. What is true, however, is that following this method over the long term will create changes in your life that will bring you a more fulfilled and happier life. The more you change within, the greater will be the changes without. It is impossible for nothing to happen. As soon as you make any change on the inside, however seemingly small it is, the omnipresent, all-powerful universe will reward you. May you manifest all you desire.

The Law of Attraction

Why is it that some people attract love and prosperity, while others do not? If you have not already achieved the things you want in your life, then this is an important question. The most general answer has to be that your beliefs are sabotaging you. And the reason this sabotage occurs is down to the power of the Law of Attraction.

The Law of Attraction is the universal law that governs what we attract into our lives – the underlying principle of the universe that brings things, events and people into our lives like a magnet. This energetic law, which states that what we attract into our lives is what we give attention to, was known by ancient spiritual traditions as diverse as Polynesian shamanism (spiritual teachings from the islands of the Pacific Ocean, including Hawaii), Tantrism (the esoteric aspect of Hinduism) and the Christian tradition. The knowledge was originally closely guarded by the 'keepers' or 'holy men' of each religion, but has now become widely known.

According to this law, the universe is made up of thought. Thought is energy and we attract into our lives those things that we think about, whether our thoughts are conscious or unconscious. The part of this to really pay attention to is the unconscious part. Your unconscious is a very powerful tool. It is a storehouse for your thoughts and emotions. If you think you want one thing in your life, but you keep attracting the opposite, it may well be that your deep, unconscious beliefs are sabotaging your plans. The thoughts you have are attached to emotions, and a strong thought plus a strong emotion will always and inevitably overrule a weak thought coupled with a weak emotion.

The Spiritual Universe

The universe as a whole is a universe of energy and thought. The energy of the spiritual universe is of a higher frequency of vibration than that of the physical universe, but they are both made up of the same basic material of energy, known by many names: aether, *qi* (*ch'i*), *mana*, *prana* or simply 'light'. Within the higher frequencies or vibrations of the universe are found spiritual helpers such as angels and other guides (see Your Spiritual Healers, pages 98–109 and Your Prosperity Helpers, pages 188–202). Your higher self, which is your invisible spiritual self, also lives in this part of the universe. Energy carries thought. Every thought you have is alive in the spiritual universe. It is then made real within the physical universe. If you think you will stay healthy, you will. If you believe that you can become rich or attract love, you will. This is the Law of Attraction. To put it simply: what you focus on is what you will create in your life. What you truly believe you are, you will become. The universe is programmed to deliver you the love you want just as soon as you prepare yourself to receive it. It precisely reflects into reality the sum total of everything you believe yourself able to be, do or have.

Do you attract into your life what you want?

Is your answer to this question a definite yes? Or do you attract 'accidentally', bringing into your life what you do not want, and repeating the same negative patterns again and again? If you are

> We attract what we give attention to, whether it is positive or negative.

not attracting the life you want, you have the power to change your life by changing your thoughts and setting out your intention for a new future. Perhaps you hold certain beliefs that say you cannot have

what you want, or you might have a deep-held belief that you don't deserve these things. Whenever you start to uncover your deeply held beliefs, unconscious as they may be, you will discover that there are many mixed thoughts and emotions in there, and that these may be at odds with the identity and beliefs that you outwardly project to the world.

Truly Believe

This idea of the universe being programmed to deliver what you want can be confusing.

There is a very simple answer to this. We attract into our lives everything we give attention to, whether it is positive or negative. All of reality exists first in the mind before it exists in your present. So if you spend ten minutes a day consciously thinking about all the happy experiences you are going to bring into your life and then spend the other 23 hours and 50 minutes unconsciously believing that this sort of experience never happens to you, guess which experience you are going to create?

The Law of Attraction works at the level of thought. We draw towards us what we really believe we are deserving of in our lives. If you believe you can find a love who will adore and cherish you, then you will manifest or draw that person into your life in reality. If you don't love yourself at a deep level, then you will unconsciously create experiences in your life that fulfil that belief that you are unlovable.

The universe is aware on a moment-by-moment basis of what you are focusing on. It is not enough just to hope and want something to happen. Your life will change at the moment you truly believe it can happen and start to imagine a new future.

Open up your life bag

In the famous Rider Waite Tarot pack, the Fool is the card numbered zero. Have you ever wondered why? It is because this figure represents us at the beginning of our journey through life. The Fool sets out on his journey not really knowing what he will encounter, an act that takes great faith. This is why the Fool is pictured stepping out over the edge of a cliff. (Doesn't it always feel a bit like that when you take your first steps into the unknown?) If you look at the picture closely, you will see that he has a little bit of room in front of him to step forward. The meaning of this is that you always have some room to move and change in your life. In the future, when you look back at the beginning of your journey, you will

notice that some of the limitations you thought you had were illusory. You always have the power to move forward.

On his back, the Fool carries a black bag. We all carry baggage with us as we go through life — it is an inevitable part of living. I think

> **If your beliefs are negative, they act as blocks to attracting good things into your life.**

the interesting thing is to open up this bag and see what is inside. That is how the Hawaiians think about it. In Hawaiian shamanism, or Huna, it is said that the unconscious mind is like a black bag. Inside this bag are all the beliefs we hold about ourselves, other people and the world in which we live. If these beliefs are negative, they act as blocks to attracting good things into your life. I have always imagined this bag to be exactly like the one on the back of the Fool, with its drawstrings tightly shut, because if the drawstrings are closed then we do not see what lies inside. If our baggage is hidden, we are often unaware of it — which is why it's important for each of us to open up our black bag to examine what is inside.

What is your belief baggage?

Do you know what is inside your baggage of beliefs? Many of us know some of the things that prevent us from making big changes in our lives, but I can also say with certainty that every client I have ever worked with as a coach has been unaware of their deeply held beliefs in their entirety and of how those beliefs affect their attraction patterns. Our deepest-held beliefs — those beliefs that really govern how we live our lives — are often unconscious. They may have been formed long, long ago when we were small children.

Do you think in the same way as other people you know? Do you share many of the same ways of thinking about the world as your family? Or perhaps as part of a wider group? If so, you may not even realize that your way of thinking is just a belief. You may call it a 'fact', rather than think of it as an opinion.

Well, if your beliefs have served you well, that is fine. Do not change what does not need changing. If something is not working in your life, however, take the opportunity to open up that black bag in your unconscious mind — the one like that on the back of the Fool — and shed some light on its contents. Once you have exposed to the light

what was previously unknown to you, it can never be concealed again inside the bag. Even if it is supposedly 'out of sight', you will still know it is there. You will now be aware of your thinking patterns, and that is the beginning of change.

Are you in 'lack' or in 'abundance'?

The thoughts and beliefs that empower you are 'abundance' beliefs. These ways of thinking allow you to create a flow of love, wealth and prosperity in your life. They give you more positive choices in life and open up greater opportunities. If you hold abundance beliefs, you feel prosperous and act as a magnet for attracting prosperity into your life.

The thoughts and beliefs that disempower you are 'lack' beliefs. These ways of thinking block you from attracting love and prosperity. In prosperity, they trap you in what is sometimes called 'poverty consciousness'. Essentially this means that, whatever you do, you do not seem to be able to create a feeling of richness and may struggle with debt or just poor money luck. Sometimes people who have a lot of wealth still retain their poverty consciousness and attract either the loss of the wealth or loss in other parts of their lives because of that wealth. Lack beliefs can make you feel poor, or they may make you anxious that you may become poor in future.

Or perhaps you are reading this book because you feel that in some way your life is missing love. You feel a lack — a gap that needs to be filled. Perhaps you miss the companionship of friends; on a deeper level you may simply miss the feeling of love.

I can think of few worse feelings than the feeling of being alone without hope of change. It is very easy for other people to tell you to keep busy or look on the bright side of life. But how do you actually pull yourself from a place of lack to a place of belief and abundance?

For what you feel right now, if it isn't love, it is most definitely lack:

* Crying over your lost relationship is lack.

* That feeling when you are by yourself at home in the evening, longing for a phone call or a friend or someone's arms around you, is lack.

* Blaming other people for your pain because they have forgotten to ask how you are, or call you or invite you out, is lack.

* Thinking that you aren't good enough, or there is something fundamentally wrong with you that pushes love away, is lack.

Are you willing to change?

Are you willing to do what it takes to bring happiness into your life? This is the starting point for all change as far as I am concerned.

Really think about the answer. Take a day or so and see what comes into your mind. Because really, let's be honest, sometimes it is much easier not to be happy and to go on doing things the way we have always done them rather than take action and make a change.

What do you do if the answer is 'no'? Well, the first thing to do is accept that this is where you are right now. Self-acceptance is the place where healing starts and ends. Once you have accepted yourself, you can move forward in a positive way to heal your old hurts and replace your old thinking habits with new ones.

What we are consciously aware of thinking about and focusing on is not always what we are really unconsciously focusing on. It may be that you have very clear wants and goals, but they don't happen. Sometimes our real beliefs about life were formed such a long time ago they are now totally outside our awareness, buried deep in our unconscious minds.

If you take the time to explore your beliefs, then you can also change them.

Lack beliefs in love:

* I don't deserve to be loved
* There is something wrong with me
* I have to be a particular type of person to be loved
* Other people get more love than me because they are better or nicer than me in some way
* I have to do or achieve something to deserve love

Lack beliefs in prosperity:

* Prosperity is just greed.
* It is morally wrong to be wealthy.
* Poor people are much nicer than rich people.
* You can be more spiritual if you are poor than if you are wealthy.
* He has more wealth than I so he can't be very nice or certainly not as nice as I am.

Inherited beliefs

Have you inherited any beliefs about love and prosperity? If so, spend some time thinking about them. Your mother or grandfather or great-grandmother may have had a set of beliefs that was formed during a very different period of history from the one in which you are living. Do you really want to carry their beliefs through the family line, or would you rather think of new ones for yourself?

The 'group mind' is also a very strong influence on our beliefs. Think about how much you were influenced into adopting certain ways of thinking about the world when you were at school. How many of your successes or failures are similar to those of your friends? Have you simply adopted a particular way of thinking that is the same as that of your peer group, profession, culture, or country? These are all powerful group mindsets.

You may have lots of ways of thinking you that are not conscious of. Some of these may protect you from harm but perhaps they also block you. Maybe there are other ways of thinking that would be more useful and still keep you safe from risk. If you never take risks, it may be time to start asking questions. For example:

* Why do I act like this? What are the thoughts that underlie my general way of acting?
* How do my current beliefs make me feel?
* What are the consequences of my current beliefs on me, on others and on my life as a whole?

You don't have to keep thinking or acting in a particular way just because that's what you have always done, or because that's how other people in your family or your friends have always done it.

Become a belief detective

Bet you didn't realize that you are already a great detective! You have spent much of your life hunting out evidence to support your current beliefs, whatever they are. As we get older we all get really good at this. We notice the things that happen to us that support our current ways of thinking. We cut out the stuff that doesn't support our current ways of thinking. Once you begin to consciously pay attention to your thinking, your unconscious mind will assist you by making you aware of what beliefs act as barriers to receiving love and prosperity. Then, in order to change what you think, hunt down the evidence to support the new beliefs you want to adopt.

> In order to change what you think, hunt down the evidence to support your new beliefs.

Are you aware what your beliefs about love are? And what about those on prosperity? As you read this book make a note of all the thoughts that occur to you about your attitudes to both love and life in general.

Envy

It seems that envy is endemic in our world right now. The media is saturated with programmes, both fictional and non-fictional, showing the lives of very affluent people.

Social media, newspapers and magazines are awash with stories of the rich and famous. Some are even devoted solely to the subject of 'celebrity' gossip and accompanying displays of wealth. When I was growing up, I thought much more about what I wanted to achieve and what I wanted to be than I did about the lives of wealthy celebrities. It must be tough these days being a child who is constantly exposed to other people's ways of life not to become dissatisfied with your own and jealous of other people who have more than you. But you need to be wary of this type of thinking. Manifesting prosperity founded on comparisons does not work well because it is a form of lack belief. If you are an envious person, you will need to examine your motivations and change your beliefs.

If you look around and say, 'I want to manifest a home like this,' you must have a clear intention to move toward abundance. If, however, you say, 'I want to have more than everyone else because I deserve it more than they do,' your intention to manifest wealth and prosperity is not coming from a place of abundance.

If you say, 'I want what they have got,' but you have envy in your heart as you say it, you are putting out negative energy to the universe. Even if you do create wealth in the short term, those negative thoughts that are attached to your goals are, inevitably, always going to backfire on you in the longer term.

Making a permanent change

As you continue reading through the manifestation process described in this book, come back again and again to check your thoughts for any limiting or blocking beliefs. Changing your thoughts for the positive and empowering yourself is the single biggest leverage you have when it comes to manifesting or not manifesting what you want. This is why exercises on changing and mapping your beliefs have been placed right at the front of this book, and they apply to manifesting both love and prosperity.

Many people like the idea of manifestation but think that changing your thoughts is not going to be easy and so they give up. Let's clear up this wrong assumption. At its very simplest, belief change is about using your imagination – if you can imagine your life differently, you can make your life different. Changing your conscious and unconscious thoughts is all about feeling better. Empowering beliefs allow you to feel happier as a natural consequence because you have more choices about the life that is available to you.

Can you imagine being someone who is happy with a life of abundance? What would your life be like if you were prosperous?

Whatever thoughts these two questions sparked off, just decide to let them become true. Begin to dream about your new life. Feed your mind with positive thoughts and happy future imaginings and notice how your mood lifts every day. If you find you need a belief booster, use any of the techniques that follow to help you keep to your dreams. The techniques and rituals in other chapters of the book are also really useful in this regard. There are a lot of different ideas to play with, not because you need to use every single one of them, but because many people find that books with one method only are too simplistic and sometimes do not fit their particular circumstances. A range of choices helps you to tailor both techniques and rituals to what works best for you, so that you can achieve optimum results.

Universal mirrors

If you suspect that you have some negative beliefs, but can't quite grasp what they are, there's another simple way to uncover them and play belief detective.

It's easy to check where you are right now in your progress towards your new life just by looking at the 'universal mirrors' around you. The universe is incredibly logical. It provides us with a very useful checklist we can keep an eye on every day.

> You'll often notice the mirrors are strongest in the people closest to you.

What are universal mirrors? Well, have you ever noticed that your friends tend to have the same problems as you do? Do you see people around you who are in some way mirroring back to you what you believe to be true about life? For example, you notice that lots of

your friends are lonely or unhappy, or have had bad relationship experiences, or get let down a lot. That could make you believe that this must just be what life is like. Actually, life doesn't have to be like that. It is just the universe mirroring back to you what you believe life to be like, in the form of what's happening around you. You'll often notice the mirrors are strongest in the people closest to you.

As soon as you start to really change your beliefs and pay attention to different thoughts and feelings, you'll start to observe very different people coming into your world. You may see a couple in a café being really loving to each other, or a group of friends out having a great time. Perhaps someone you know, who has had a hard time in the past, will suddenly have a breakthrough. Take these as signs of change in your universe.

My mirrors

Think about the people to whom you are closest on a daily basis. What do you think their beliefs are? What do you think they believe to be true about the world? About love? And prosperity? About being in a couple? About being wealthy? About anything else relevant to what you would like to change in your life?

Be honest with yourself. How much of what you have written down could apply to you?

Mapping Beliefs

One trick I have learned from neuro-linguistic programming (NLP) is to map beliefs visually on paper. Write down each belief in turn, then join them together to make a belief tree or flow chart. You can put arrows from one belief to another to show which belief flows out of another belief or gives rise to more

> If you undo a deep belief, you may undo several others.

than one thought. By doing this you will begin to see patterns – some beliefs are much deeper than others. If you undo a deep belief you will probably undo several other beliefs at the same time. This is because when we accept an idea as a fact, we then go through life looking for evidence to support it and adopt other beliefs as a consequence. If you can get rid of a deep belief, then the whole belief 'cluster' will disappear. This is why it is important to hunt out evidence to undo the deepest beliefs, and indeed to become aware of any that we are not already aware of.

Draw your belief tree

Draw your belief tree on the biggest piece of paper you can find. Draw in as many branches of your beliefs as you can think of. You will get great satisfaction as you disprove your limiting or lack beliefs and cross out some of the branches or draw in fresh branches with new, empowering beliefs.

You may find it easier to shake up your thinking by drawing two trees to begin with – the first is the limiting belief tree, the second the empowering or abundance belief tree. The second tree does not have to be limited to only the beliefs you have now, but can also include beliefs you would like to take on. Place your belief trees next to each other, so that you can see them side by side. This will get your unconscious really thinking about the benefits of one versus the other.

Put the limiting belief tree on the left or below the empowering belief tree. This is because, for many of us, we see the future in our mind's eye as running to the right or in front of us. It is a little trick, but actually works remarkably well to stimulate the unconscious mind.

Now, the Law of Attraction works not just according to our thoughts, but also due to the emotions we have that are connected with these thoughts. If you are clear about which emotions are connected with which particular beliefs on your belief tree, map these as well. You will find that your limiting belief tree contains all sorts of negative emotions. Your empowering belief tree, on the other hand, will contain all sorts of happy and positive emotions. This contrast is a great motivation for the unconscious to make any necessary changes.

Stop to look at each tree and the beliefs (and emotions) that they represent...

Really think about one versus the other and take time to notice how much easier and more pleasant it is to look at the empowering tree versus the limiting tree.

Once you have convinced yourself of the need to change, begin to look for evidence that the empowering beliefs are true (for you as an individual, as well as in general) and that they are the best way forward in your life.

If you need an extra convincer, it is sometimes fun to add to your limiting belief map where these beliefs have come from — family, groups etc. Make the decision to let go of any old family or group patterns and take on board new

My Belief Tree

My conscious beliefs about love or prosperity

My core belief about love or prosperity

beliefs that are suitable for who you are now. Remind yourself that it would be ridiculous, for example, to carry the same way of thinking about the world as a great-grandparent who lived in a different century.

Summary

Thought is the driver of the Law of Attraction. It is vital that you know and understand yourself well enough to be aware of any thoughts, conscious or unconscious, that might block you being able to manifest prosperity.

It doesn't matter where you are right now. It really doesn't matter what has happened up to now in your life. The starting point to attracting what you want into your life is precisely where you are right now. The past is the past. The future is a new chapter waiting to be written as you read this guide and begin to put some of what you learn into practice.

Take the time to examine your thinking. What mindset have you inherited or taken on throughout your lifetime? Why is it that you are not already where you want to be? What are your blocking or limiting beliefs? As you do this, be aware of the emotions triggered by your beliefs. What evidence can you find for more abundant and enabling beliefs? As you consider this, start to imagine another life – the life of your dreams. Notice how much happier and lighter you feel. Over the next days, weeks and months, examine and work with your beliefs and find the evidence you need to enable you to manifest your intentions.

As martial arts expert and movie star Bruce Lee is reported to have said, 'I fear not the man who has practised ten thousand kicks once, but I fear the man who has practised one kick ten thousand times.' In other words, keep doing something again and again, and it becomes a habit – a very powerful habit indeed, because it becomes an entirely unconscious skill.

As you carry on reading, just begin your new future by starting to become aware of your thought patterns. It is very simple. Pay attention softly to the kind of thoughts you have. Begin to notice when you catch your thoughts from time to time, where you are thinking thoughts of lack rather than loving and abundant thoughts. When you catch yourself in lack, just make a mental note. There is no need to tell yourself off or anything else. For the moment just be aware.

Manifesting

*

LOVE

1: Heal Your Past

'Keep walking, though there's no place
to get to. Don't try to see through the
distances. That's not for human beings.'

Rumi

In this chapter you will learn ways in which to heal negative emotions connected to your past relationships. Negative emotions can get in the way of attracting love as the vibration of anger, guilt or sadness is stored at a cellular level in your body. Negative emotions remain as blocks in your unconscious, causing you to attract the same old patterns and people until they are healed and cleared away.

There are many different ways to heal your past. You can use spiritual rituals, meditation, neuro-linguistic programming (NLP), trance, body work or magical techniques. They are all designed to do one thing – stop you filling your energy with 'lack' (see page 14) caused by negative thinking so that you create a space for positivity, laughter, fun, joy and, of course, love attraction.

In this chapter you will learn:

* What your love résumé can teach you
* How to identify the roles you play in your life and to let go of unhelpful past roles
* How to heal hurt and the Hawaiian practice of forgiveness – a method you can use to help yourself heal

Lucy's Journey

After ten years of marriage, Lucy found out that her husband had been having an affair, not only all the time they had been married, but all the time they had been dating. She was devastated. It took her several months to come to terms with what had happened. She was scared of being alone and bringing up their children by herself, but eventually, Lucy asked him to leave.

The whole experience really broke her heart. Lucy had a 'relationship drought period' of over ten years

> There are many different ways to heal your past.

while her children were growing up. She did date from time to time and had a couple of short-lived boyfriends. At the same time she found it very hard to trust any man fully enough to let go and commit to a longer relationship of the type she had had before she met her husband. 'I didn't know that I couldn't commit or trust,' Lucy says. 'If you had asked me over the last few years, I would have said there was nothing I wanted more than someone to fall in love with and to fall in love with me. But part of me never believed it was possible.'

Lucy's story is one that many of us have experienced in similar ways. Once you have been knocked by an unhappy childhood or bad love experiences, it is so easy just to let go of the belief that it is possible to find true love. We may long to fall in love but, at the same time, all those old hurts are telling us that we will just get hurt again. If you want to change this pattern then it is important to understand why you attracted these experiences to begin with.

Fear of change

Some people have only one fear, and that is fear of change. Even though they haven't got exactly what they want in life, and they aren't comfortable, they aren't too uncomfortable. They fear, for example, that because having a relationship hurt them in the past, it might hurt again, so by not trying to attract love at least they can avoid misery.

There's a story that relates how there was a man who was afraid of lots of things. He was worried that the earth would collapse and swallow him up. He was afraid that the sky would collapse one day and fall on top of him. The more and more he thought about all the things that could happen to him, the more he worried. It got to the point when he was too afraid to sleep in case something terrible happened while he was in bed. Then a friend took him aside and explained that he could keep living in fear if he wanted to, but really his fears were groundless. He explained that earth is just dirt and the sky is just air. Air is light and couldn't hurt him. The earth had never cracked. Why should it crack now?

It is easy to imagine all the things that can happen that are bad, but why bother? Why not simply forget about those possibilities, change focus and work out what you want to bring into your life instead that is happy and fun and exciting and loving?

You always have the choice, no matter what, to refuse to be ruled by fear, guilt, blame or any other negative emotion you have learned. You were born a loving creature who was meant to be a love attractor. Babies assume they will be loved and looked after. There is no need for you as an adult to be any different. You were once a natural love attractor. You can and will be again. You can take a practical step forward through your fear by looking at your past so you can heal it.

Your love résumé

Writing a love résumé is a good place to start. A résumé is a way of tweaking out any thoughts about love within relationships. It serves several purposes. It is a summary of your past experience and it shows all your skills and achievements.

You may already have a career résumé — something you typically sit down and write only when you are ready to move on to another job. You sit down and work out what skills you have that your future employer might want.

Well, a love résumé isn't that different. It's a way of thinking about all your past experiences and learning from them so that you can move forward to something better in the future. In the same way you have to think about your career, writing a love résumé gives you the opportunity to think about everything you want to keep in your life and everything you want to discard.

What does your love résumé look like? A little patchy? Full of lovely experiences and people you have met in the past? Or does it contain some experiences that you would rather not repeat in the future?

Unlike your career résumé, you're not going to show your love résumé to anyone, but it is going to help you to change your future relationships as long as you write everything down. A written love résumé lets you be very objective about what has and hasn't worked in the past.

Exercise

Write a love résumé

* Jot down on a piece of paper a list of all the relationships you have had up to now. Write down the specifics, times and dates.

* Then take a long look at what you have written. Notice what sort of situations and people you have attracted to you in the past. Perhaps you have some themes running through your résumé? If so, make a note of what you think they are.

* Write down any beliefs that you think you would like to change. You can use the belief change process on pages 12–21 to challenge and change these.

* Next think about yourself in relation to these relationships. What beliefs and ways of thinking in you attracted these relationships to you? Remember that the Law of Attraction works on a 'like attracts like' principle.

* Now look at your experiences in the past. Just as you would if you were thinking about your career, be objective. There will be some things you have experienced in the past that you would like to experience again: What do you want to keep? What characteristics of the person in the past, or your life together, worked for you?

* Make a separate list of the features of relationships that you would like to keep in the next relationship you have – and perhaps have even more of.

Think in positive language

Having done your love résumé, it is important from now on to focus on what worked rather than what didn't work, so that you can attract more of what you want. The Law of Attraction doesn't process negatives. If you think, 'I don't want rejection', it hears the word 'rejection' and brings you more of it. Instead of thinking, 'I don't want any more of a man/woman who forgets to give me presents', turn

> Focus on what worked rather than what didn't work.

your thinking around and say to yourself: 'I liked the fact he/she remembered my birthday. Now I would like even more fun, shared hobbies, romantic evenings together, Sunday dinners, intelligent talk, laughter and presents', then you will start attracting more abundance into your life.

Identify the roles you play

True love is unconditional. Unconditional love is abundant. It frees you up to have choices in your life. When you are in a really loving relationship, you will feel more of yourself, not less of yourself. However, holding on to negative feelings results in us playing roles rather than letting love flow freely. Look back at your love résumé. How many of the following roles, if any, have you played in the past?

Role One: The Judge

Your inner judge is the part of you that passes sentence on you. You'll know if you have an inner judge because it will tell you that you are not good enough, a bad person and not worthy, and will sentence you to the punishment of a life without unconditional love.

A judge is unforgiving, not only of self, but also of others. If you feel very bad about yourself you may find that you are very harsh about other people as well, as a way of deflecting attention from yourself.

However, as the old saying goes: 'one finger points out, three fingers point back'. If you pass judgement on other people you get it back threefold. If you pass love to other people you get it back threefold. Whatever we project to the world we receive back. If you are judging the behaviour of other people it is because inside you feel a victim.

Role Two: The Victim

The victim is the part of you who thinks events and other people are responsible for what happens to you in life. A victim feels powerless and helpless. A victim doesn't feel they have the freedom to choose their own life.

A love victim attracts relationships where other people dump them or treat them badly. They do not feel they have the power to show themselves as they really are because they are afraid of bullying, abuse and attack.

I am sure you have met a number of victims in your life. You may even have been one yourself on occasion. Yes, I know it's embarrassing to admit it, but many of us do like sympathy when we have ended a relationship or during a relationship. The trouble is that while we may get a bit of sympathy, we don't get love. This is not a love-attraction pattern that works because it is founded on lack beliefs rather than loving beliefs.

If you are a victim, then you lack one thing in addition to love and that is hope. The part of you that is a victim feels not worthy to receive love. It feels in some way to blame for the fact that it can't receive the love it wants. So it doesn't expect that things will change. The Law of Attraction works on expectation, so if any part of you is a victim experiencing these feelings, then you won't attract love to you.

If you are still not sure whether you have adopted the victim role in the past, then think about the following questions.

* Do you blame yourself for the fact that you haven't attracted the love you want yet?
* Do you feel that you aren't good enough in some way?
* Do you feel ashamed about anything and therefore feel unworthy of real love?

If you say 'yes' to any of these questions, then you are playing out victim lack patterns in your life. The beliefs that underlie the 'yes' are all untruths.

Letting go of Judge and Victim

It is time to let go of self-judgement once and for all. Judging yourself, blaming yourself and feeling guilty all destroy the love magnet within you because they destroy self-acceptance.

The less you beat yourself up, the more you accept yourself and the more love you feel. The more love you feel, the more lovable you become.

Do you deserve love? The only true answer here is 'yes'. We all deserve love. We are all worthy of love. We are all good enough. We are all born to receive unconditional love. If you feel that something inside you is not deserving of love, it is a lie that you have learned. Healing all the hurts you have carried from the past lets you live your life so that your love begins to expand.

Healing the hurt

Just stop for a moment. Notice, if you are carrying negative feelings, where they are in your body. This is something I first learned from Tibetan Buddhism, but it has been taken up by non-spiritual practitioners such as exponents of neuro-linguistic programming as well. When you feel an emotion you may feel it as a tightness, a change in temperature, or even as a moving feeling within your stomach, chest or another part of your body.

Think about fear. Think about blame or guilt. Where are you carrying these emotions? Feelings have a texture to them, they carry an energy charge that can be felt as hot or cold. You feel a feeling because it is an energy within the cells of your body. Each time you express the pain you do so in order to make it go away, but instead it actually makes it stay — stored in your body.

Next time you start feeling that you are a judge or victim and notice all the negative emotions that come out of those patterns of behaviour, think about how you are carrying all those emotions in your body and what they are doing to you:

* Instead of beating yourself up, simply say: 'No one is to blame here' and let it go.

* Instead of feeling guilty for not being perfect, simply say: 'Well, no one is perfect, so who cares. I am fine as I am.'

* Instead of pointing the finger at the boyfriend or girlfriend who didn't behave in the way you hoped or expected, simply say: 'They did the best they could at the time and so did I.'

* Instead of saying: 'There must be something wrong with me or things would have worked out better', simply say: 'Who cares' or 'There's always a next time'.

* Instead of saying: 'He/she is a bad person', simply say: 'This is what I did love about them. This is what I learned from the experience and this is what I am going to ask for more of next time.'

* Instead of punishing yourself as a judge so that you can play the victim, forgive yourself. Be kind. We spend so much time beating ourselves up that we often forget to be kind. Relax. Let it go.

Forgiveness

Ask the universe what you need to learn from the experiences you have had in the past. If there is pain or loss or hurt, then ask what you need to learn to let go of these feelings.

* Forgive your past boyfriends.
* Forgive your past girlfriends.
* Forgive the friends who have hurt you.
* Forgive your parents.
* Forgive yourself.

Even though it may seem unfair to forgive, ultimately every time you forgive another person you are actually helping yourself. On an energetic level we are all joined together. The image of another person you carry inside you with all those negative feelings attached to it is part of you. When you forgive that person, you get rid of the negative energy within yourself.

Forgiveness is the easiest path to love. Every time you forgive yourself, you bless those cells in your body that were filled with pain. You allow them to leave your body. You thank them for how they have served you and then you let go.

Every time you let go of a bad experience and move on, you clear out pain and hurt and make space for love.

Hawaiian practices of love and forgiveness

Before other people will show you love, you must discover your own self as a hidden treasure. The ritual below is a wonderful way of beginning this process.

I first visited Hawaii 15 years ago to study Hawaiian shamanism, a spiritual tradition that is possibly 35,000 years old. Some people believe that the islands of Hawaii are equivalent to the seven chakras of our planet (see page 43), acting as core energy points for the Earth. In Hawaii shamans are known as *kahunas* — a name that originally probably meant a master or doctor and evolved to mean a priest or magician. Over the years *kahunas* have been psychics, healers and even shamans who were said to be able to influence the weather.

The ancient teachings of Hawaii are known as 'Huna', which translates as 'the secret'. It is likely that much of Huna wisdom is still secret, as different Huna traditions were guarded within the islands and lineages of Hawaii.

It is only relatively recently that Huna has been studied outside the islands and become more open within them.

Hawaiian forgiveness ritual

Huna teaches that one of the most important things you can do is to practise forgiveness. This isn't a new message. Forgiveness is key to every great spiritual tradition, but within the Huna tradition forgiveness is part of what is known as the Huna Prayer, a method of manifesting. Forgiving others, preferably as a daily practice, is actually a way of forgiving yourself and of self-healing.

Huna can also be translated to mean the perfect balance of feminine and masculine, or yin and yang. *Hu* means masculine and *ha* feminine. Every Huna practice brings the two poles together and ourselves into balance. In Huna the forgiveness practice is known as ho' o' pono pono, which means 'to make things right/balanced' (*pono*). The practice of forgiveness heals you energetically and brings you into balance. A balanced person is full of self-love and ready to attract love from everyone, including from a romantic partner.

Love and harmony

The ancient Hawaiians understood that in order to attract love we need first to be happy and healed within ourselves. You can't participate in a loving relationship with another person if you can't love yourself.

Love and harmony are inseparable in the Huna spiritual tradition. The word for love in Hawaiian is *aloha*. *Ha* means the breath of life, *alo* means to be with and *oha* means happiness. Together these sounds are used as a loving welcome because the ancient Hawaiians greeted others with love. When you say *aloha* to someone you are telling them you want to share happiness and joy with them. Spiritually, you understand that everything you do touches someone else. Your energy directly attracts other energies of the same vibration. If you have inner happiness you will magnetize happy people towards you. You won't need to seek out love; it will naturally be drawn towards you by your energy.

Energetic cords

Every time you make a connection with someone you send an energetic cord from your energy body towards them. A connection is any kind of contact, including a simple thought about that other person or any kind of emotional connection. You have energy cords to and from people you are related to, including ancestors, people you are friends with, people you work with and people you have loved or had intimate relations with. Sometimes it is useful to disconnect and reconnect with these people, or simply to disconnect the cords so that you establish new relationships with them. After you have disconnected, you will find that your relationship feels very different to both of you — always in a positive way, when you have done this process lovingly.

Perform the Hawaiian forgiveness

The process of *ho' o' pono pono* ('Making things right') is very simple. It is something you can do on a daily basis.

* Simply sit somewhere you won't be distracted and quieten your mind.

* Imagine that you have a small stage in front of you. You can call on to that stage anyone from your life that you have unresolved issues with – perhaps ex-lovers or family members. Anybody whose image you hold in your mind with anger or grief, or any other negative emotion, is a drain on your inner love and happiness.

* Hold these images in your mind's eye on your stage with love. The easiest way to do this is to surround them with the white loving light of the universe. The energy of the universe vibrates with infinite love and healing. 'Infinite' means that the love will never be scarce. There is enough to heal anything.

* Imagine the top of your head (the crown chakra, see page 43) opening up to let this loving – healing light flow down through your whole body, filling it up so much that it pours out through your heart on to the people on the stage, filling them with love and healing.

* Say what you need to say to them. Hear what they need to say to you. Forgive them in your mind and thank them for what they have given you. Hear them forgive you for the unwitting projections or harm you have done to them.

* If you find this difficult, just remember that the people you see in your mind's eye are part of you. These images are in your unconscious, and holding on to any negative feelings only harms you. Forgiving others and letting go of these feelings is really a process of forgiving yourself for the experiences you went through. Let go and you will lift the dark spots in your unconscious, making way for light and joy and love.

* When you have completed the forgiveness process, say thank you to the people on the stage. Imagine a scythe of white light cutting the energetic cords that have kept you bound to each other. Let the cords return to whom they belong, bringing back to you all the energy that has been wasted on negativity so that it is transmuted into love and light once again. Then the people are free to leave.

* If the images are of people who are still in your life, this doesn't necessarily mean that you have to let go of contact with those people. Any time you think of them again you restore a connection with them. However, because you have let go of the negative energies, the fresh connection will be lighter, more loving and more balanced than before.

* You can repeat this process as often as you like and you will find it gets easier and easier. It clears the path of any blocks to manifesting the life you want, including the love you want.

Summary

You don't need to play roles any more in your relationships. Playing a role, being victim or judge, won't get you the relationship you both want or truly do deserve to have. Importantly it isn't a way of attracting love to you. Playing a role may get you some short-term sympathy, but it will also drive other people away.

Love is attracted by you being your true self — the perhaps vulnerable, but certainly lovable you.

You don't need to be ruled by what has happened to you in the past. Instead you can choose to let go of any bad feelings you have about your past. You can let go of bad feelings about past relationships, past friendships that have hurt you and any other past hurts. By forgiving what has happened to you in the past and taking charge of how you focus on your past, you will start to feel differently. You will create different energy around you and a space into which love can flow once more.

You can use the techniques in this chapter to help you to heal any past hurts. By doing this you will banish negative patterns of behaviour and create a fresh, energetically neutral starting point from which to begin to manifest a different and loving future.

2: Fall in Love With Yourself

'You, yourself, as much as anybody in
the entire universe, deserve your love
and affection.'

Buddha

When you make changes in your everyday life on a practical
level you will start to feel differently about yourself; your body
language will change, the things you say will change. When you
change on the inside, people will begin to react differently to you
and the experiences you attract into your life will change.
Learning to love yourself is a vital step towards attracting love
from others into your life.

In this chapter you will learn:

* About the key belief that supports love
* How to dance on the inside: love your body, your mind and
  the inner you
* How to open your heart chakra and give love to the world
* About heart-to-heart cords and the difference between
  sex and love

Love yourself first

I often meet people who are baffled as to why they haven't attracted loving friends or a loving partner into their life. 'I am such a nice person,' they say. 'Look at that person over there. They are not nearly as nice as me. I help people out, I do good deeds. I am always helpful to others, so why don't people ring me up or invite me out? Why don't I have a special person in my life who loves me? If you put other people first without really loving yourself at the same time, you won't attract lasting love. The Law of Attraction acts on a 'like attracts like' basis, so the people who come into your life will have the same issues about love as you.

When you don't love yourself, then you can't really love another person. Instead you feel an addiction or a need to be with that person, to know what they are doing and to control their actions so that they can't leave you.

The key love belief

There is one belief that people who attract love easily have about themselves: 'I am perfect just as I am.' The truth is we are all born perfect. You just need to look at yourself and recognize that fact. We are all born to be loved. You don't need to do anything to attract other people to you, other than recognize the love within yourself.

Love doesn't come by you trying to force it or by you striving to make it happen. Love is already there inside you. It reveals itself when you begin to nourish yourself. All manifestation in the material world starts by you working on yourself on the inside. You will only create change externally when you have first created change internally. How much do you love yourself? If you don't love yourself, how can you expect others to fall in love with you?

In this chapter I am going to show you how to embark on a journey of self-discovery to fall in love with yourself so that you can open your heart to receiving more love from others. The secret really is so simple: love yourself and you will attract love. Change happens when you love the whole of you – inside and outside.

So let's look at some steps you can take.

Become entrancing

Have you ever noticed any of these things happening to you when you are in love?

* You notice wonderful details about another person or the world around you

* Time feels as if it is passing at a different rate

* Your senses become heightened – the world feels and looks richer and more vibrant, perhaps more exciting

If the answer is 'yes', it's because you are in a love trance. In a love trance we cut out all the negative 'chatter' around us and focus only on the good things. It is a wonderful feeling – like going around in your own blissful little bubble.

When we fall in love we become entranced by the person we are in love with. We find everything about them delightful, even mesmerizing. I have chosen my words very carefully here. The word

> **Embark on a journey of self-discovery; fall in love with yourself and open your heart to receiving love from others.**

'mesmerizing' comes from the name of the physician, Franz Mesmer, who theorized in the late 18th/early 19th century about mesmerism, the forerunner of hypnosis. He was able to put people into a trance through just his words and actions. When you are in a trance you are in a different state, noticing different things about yourself or other people than you would in your normal state of mind. If you have ever seen people on stage in a hypnosis show, you'll have seen very

clearly how they can be guided to behave differently from usual. I am not suggesting that you need believe that you are a chicken, or go and do a headstand against the wall, as you may have seen in a hypnosis show, but do something much more useful – become entranced by yourself!

Actually, if you have ever tried any form of meditation or self-hypnosis, or any other kind of trance induced by shamanistic drumming or deep-breathing practices like rebirthing, you will recognize these descriptions of being entranced. The word 'entrance' makes you think of 'being delightful, wonderful and beautiful to yourself and others' as well as 'being in a trance'. When you go into a trance state you can create the love vibration that will not only make you notice all the good things about yourself, but will also attract love from other people.

What I want to happen to you while you read this book is that you fall deeply in love with yourself. Be open to the possibility that it could happen quite quickly, if not suddenly out of the blue, because that is how love often strikes. You'll know when it has happened because you will start to dance on the inside. You will feel a sense of joy about yourself that will feel strangely familiar, really because it is not new but just remembering what you were born to believe about yourself.

Love the inner 'you' behind the mask

There is a Buddhist tale about the man who goes searching for happiness. No matter where he looks he can't find it because it has been hidden in the one place we always forget to look — deep inside ourselves.

We all have masks. A mask is the identity we show to the world and to ourselves.

Sometimes we are aware that we are putting on a mask and sometimes we are not. Sometimes we forget we are wearing masks and think we are that person.

Many of us do this when we are embarking on a new relationship because, if we haven't had much luck in the past, we think we have to pretend to be someone different to win our date over.

Have you ever walked into a party and put on a false front? Have you ever been on a date and pretended to be interested in things you weren't, or be someone you aren't? The trouble with this approach is that you won't be able to keep it up for very long. When you let the mask slip, your date will realize that you are a different person and that's often too much of a shock. Then, if the date goes wrong, you think it's because you showed yourself. Actually it is because you didn't show yourself early enough.

When you really love yourself from the inside there is no need to wear a big mask anymore. Be who you are. I don't care if you are a little whacky or a bit unusual or slightly geeky. It really doesn't matter if you are so lazy that you get up late every day, or like collecting newts, or never pick the clothes up off your floor or wear the same clothes three days in a row. Honestly, there is someone out there who won't care. There are probably lots of people out there who won't care. More than that, they will actually love you even more because you have a few peculiarities and differences.

In some of the happiest couples I have seen, one or both people are a little bit grumpy, or unsocial or different in another way. Yet the more you get to know them, the more you realize how attractive this honesty is.

Love the outer you

Many of us spend too much time every day thinking about what's wrong with us on the outside. This isn't helped by the media, which talk about celebrities' appearances obsessively, commenting on the slightest pimple, sign of baldness or cellulite as if the poor person in question has committed a terrible sin by not conforming to some abstract idea of perfection. It's therefore not surprising if you look at yourself in the mirror occasionally and feel dissatisfied. However, from a Law of Attraction point of view, this isn't a helpful thing to do. All those people out there in the world who are reading magazines and comparing themselves with some airbrushed celebrity are operating out of lack.

Of course, all of us do it from time to time – think we aren't pretty enough, are too fat or too thin, have the wrong colour of hair, are of the wrong height or the wrong age. It seems quite harmless, doesn't it? But it isn't really. After all, you wouldn't tell children that they are ugly. You wouldn't tell children that they need to dye their hair, or have a nose operation. You would probably even think it abusive if you caught an adult telling a child these things not just once, but every day, or even several times a day? I would, yet I have to admit I say things to myself that I would never dream of saying to a child. The truth is, when I look at young children, whatever they look like I really only notice how perfect they are.

In reality, the majority of faces are fascinating. Yes, bodies come in all shapes and sizes and some of us have more wrinkles than others, but does that make us less perfect? The more I have thought about this over the years, the more I notice how

you can find beauty in anybody at any age. I was once told by a film director the secret of why we love Hollywood stars. It's because the camera lingers over every feature. It doesn't matter whether the star is youthful or an older character actor. The camera allows us to look at their faces close up, lingering on each of them. The only other time we get to look at someone that closely for that long is if the other person is your lover, child or parent. In other words, the reason we find these stars so fascinating to look at is because the camera gives us permission to look at them properly and thus we discover we love them. We love every imperfection, every little bit of their face. It's such a mesmeric process that just by

Learn to become entranced with yourself.

looking at an actor in this way can redefine our views on beauty. A star like Gerard Depardieu is probably a case in point. By staring at his unusual features again and again we begin to notice that these kinds of features are as compellingly attractive as daintier, more uniform features.

So next time you catch sight of yourself in the mirror, linger a while. Give yourself the attention you would give to a face in a movie. Let yourself notice how fascinating each part of your face and body is. Become entranced with yourself in the way you become entranced with a lover you are with for the first time.

Begin to love your life

Think about what makes you happy in life generally. What makes you feel alive? What makes you laugh? What brings you joy? If you have been in the habit of focusing on what doesn't make you happy – all that lack and loneliness and discomfort from not feeling loved enough – it takes some retraining to keep feeling happy on a daily basis.

Acknowledging and starting to let go of 'wrong thinking' as we have already explored is a great place to begin. Actually, taking action to do more things you enjoy every day will accelerate your progress and bring your focus more and more towards joy. Every time you feel happy and light in yourself, you raise your energy vibration and begin to attract better and better experiences towards you.

Tip the happiness balance

Think about your average day at the moment. What do you do? Get up at a certain time? Eat breakfast,

lunch and an evening meal? Go to work? Watch TV? Or stay at home? If you don't have love in your life right now, then it is time to inject a bit of joy and excitement into your routine.

Often it is having too much of a routine that is the issue itself. We all need a bit of change and excitement and spontaneity to shake us up from time to time. Sameness and structure are great supports for people, but we'd all still be living in caves if it wasn't for difference and change.

What could you do that would be fun, spontaneous, maybe a bit daring? Of course it depends on the person and how daring their life is to begin with. Take some people I know: Lydia craved a big adventure after her divorce, so one day she took off to South America to work for a charity for three months; Nicki decided to take up dancing even though, at the age of 60, she had thought she was a bit old to do anything new; Janet's new fun activity was staying in on a Friday night and cooking for girlfriends.

It really doesn't matter what other people think. The point is that you decide how much of a change to your routine is going to shake things up and tip the happiness balance in your favour.

What do you want to do? Run around the park playing with your dog, set off on a round-the-world trip, take up belly dancing, go and see live comedy, make homemade chocolates, write a book, lie in the sun or just get out of your chair and move more?

80 / 20

Make a list of the top things that you love. I always work on the 80/20 principle. If you do the most important 20 per cent regularly, then you will tip your happiness balance in your favour by 80 per cent. You don't have to do everything on the list, just the things that make the biggest difference.

If you are still not sure what to do, make a promise to yourself to lighten up. Let go of all the unimportant stuff in your life. Don't cling on to hurts.

Remember always to have a sense of humour. If on the odd occasion — and let's face it, all of us have them — you can't manage to laugh in the face of bad luck or a dull day, keep curious. That will always direct your mind away from what you don't want and towards what you do. Always maintain a joyful mind. There is only one measure of your success and that's how you feel. As soon as you begin to feel lighter, to feel happier, to feel more excited, to feel calmer, to feel that you enjoy your life more, it is working.

Every time you catch yourself having this feeling of loving your life, then it is going to make you into a love-attraction magnet, feeling more and more love as if the happiness in you is calling out across the universe to lovers and friends to come into your life now.

Opening your heart

If you have been living in lack for a while you may have constructed energetic defences around your heart.

Your heart chakra (see opposite) needs to be able to open up freely to attract love. Sometimes our chakras get blocked. If you look at a Kirlian, or energy, photograph of a person, you can see that someone who is emotionally and spiritually balanced has clear, beautifully coloured chakras going in a straight line up the front of the body. In a person who is unhappy, depressed or unbalanced in another way, some of these colours may be barely visible. Some chakras may be much more dominant than others. A balanced, loving heart looks pink or green. When it is open, the energy swirls around and looks like a bright flower opening up.

If you are not experiencing either receiving or giving love easily, then take the time to focus on the health of your heart chakra. This is a really simple process and you can spend just a few minutes on it whenever you remember.

Chakras

The word 'chakra' comes from Sanskrit and means a wheel. It generally refers to the seven energy centres, which regulate the flow of energy through and around the human body. The seven chakras are each associated with a different colour and are located on a point that corresponds to a part of the physical body (see diagram below).

Chakras are part of the energy system, which keeps us healthy not just on a physical level, but also on an emotional, spiritual and mental level. When a chakra is healthy and balanced, we are healthy. If the flow of energy within the chakra is disturbed, you will find that you become ill or affected negatively in some way on a physical or other level. If you have suffered a lot of hurt in love, this will affect the balance of your chakras and can be detected by someone with psychic skills.

Learning to open and close your chakras at will is part of the meditation practices in this book, which will help you learn to attract love into your life.

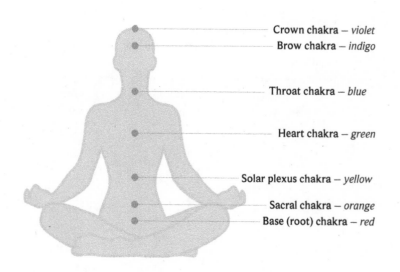

Crown chakra – *violet*
Brow chakra – *indigo*

Throat chakra – *blue*

Heart chakra – *green*

Solar plexus chakra – *yellow*

Sacral chakra – *orange*
Base (root) chakra – *red*

Exercise

Open up your heart chakra

* Imagine that your heart chakra is like a flower with petals that can open or close. Eastern traditions use the lotus as a symbol.

* See in your mind's eye the petals of the flower opening to receive all the love that is out there in the universe, and also to give love. When you give, though, see energy flowing down through the top of your head and your crown chakra and out through your heart, so that you always draw on universal energy, which never runs out.

* Then use this image from a Buddhist-derived tradition called 'heart yoga'. Imagine that you have a diamond, a most precious thing. See the diamond in the lotus of your heart and feel its joy and beauty. Let it stay there, radiating beauty and love. Let it radiate love out towards you, filling your whole energy body with love. Let it radiate love out towards the world. Know that there is always enough love to draw upon any time it is needed.

Flow your love to the universe

When your love for yourself is full, there will always be enough for you to give out to the universe. Compassion for other people is held up in many spiritual traditions as an integral part of being a loving person. Giving love abundantly boosts your energetic link with the flow of love in the universe. It reminds you that love is an energy to be shared and that we all deserve.

There is a traditional way of thinking in Tibetan Buddhism that teaches you to be compassionate by suggesting that you treat all people as your parent. When you walk around, look at strangers and thin: This person is my mother or my father. Take a look at the people you come into contact with every day. Look at the woman on the bus who is having an argument about the fare and holding you up when you are in a hurry. Can you think of her as your mother? Look at the man on the news who robbed a shop. Can you think of him as your father? Look at your neighbours who keep you awake at night playing loud music. Can you think of them as your parents?

All the great spiritual traditions tell us that we are not separate from other people, but connected. When you send out love to other people it comes back to you.

Heart cords

As we have already discussed how every time you think about someone, an energetic cord extends from your energy body to the other person (see page 32). Likewise when they think about you, an energy cord extends from them to you. Where in the energy body the link happens is key to what it feels like.

When you love another person with your heart, you send out an energetic cord from your heart to their heart. This love empowers both of you. It feels intimate and permissive and non-judgemental. This is very different from love that comes from need or co-dependence. If you could actually see energetic cords and looked at two people bound together through need rather than love, then you would literally see the binding. The energetic cords between them wouldn't be a straight cord from heart to heart, but might appear as a cord wrapping around each other like a straitjacket to keep the other person locked in. If you obsess over another person, this is what the cords look like.

Love is more permissive than this. It doesn't seek to lock the other person in and keep them bound to you, but simply stays as a heart connection. This enables each of you to live your own life and be your own person while feeling loved and supported by that love.

The difference between sex and love

It is also important not to confuse sex and love. The reason that many spiritual traditions have rules about sexual conduct is because of the over-bonding that can result through sex. Cords are attached between the two of you, but if these are not heart cords, they can drain you energetically. The more sexual connections you have that are not love connections, the more you are putting out energy that doesn't bring back love into yourself. It is important to clear non-loving connections of any sort as a way of bringing real love into your life through the Law of Attraction. The Hawaiian forgiveness ritual (see pages 31–34) is a very useful way for you to start doing this.

Summary

Love attracts love. We are all meant to be loved. We are all lovable. What stops us attracting love is not recognizing this. Attracting love from other people starts with self-love. There may be many reasons you don't recognize that you are worthy of this love. Many of us are damaged by other people's words or actions in childhood or later in life. However, you have the power to look at yourself with fresh eyes at any time of your life and see the real you free from any false ideas you may have adopted about yourself. You can find love in yourself and, when you do so, you can begin to receive love from others. Love is a habit. Love comes out of both thought and action. You can connect with love any time by being gentler with yourself, by being more compassionate with yourself and by being kind to others. Most of all, make a decision today. Decide, whether you fully believe it right now or not, to recognize that you are perfect. Be as kind to yourself as you would be to a small baby. Find in yourself that deep love for the unique you. You will start to notice how you are rewarded as you begin these new loving habits. Not only will you feel better about yourself and your life, but other people will begin to behave differently to you as well.

3: Decide Your Loving Future

'Nothing is more powerful than habit.'

Ovid

What kind of future do you want? It is time to decide so that you can create your future intentionally rather than by default. Think about what a life of love will look and feel like. The clearer you become about what you want to create, the happier you will be with the results.

In this chapter you will learn how to:

* Decide what you want and create an intention to have it

* Create a 'love treasure map' so that you can begin to dream about your new life

* Create your personal 'love list' through which you can attract new types of relationship, which will help you keep your sense of self

* Use your emotions to guide you to keep on track

Philippe Petit

One day in August 1974, something extraordinary happened. The people of New York's Lower Manhattan were going about their ordinary business. There was nothing to indicate that it was a special day, but hundreds of feet above their heads, a man was walking on a cable between the Twin Towers of the World Trade Center.

The man who made this amazing tightrope walk was Philippe Petit, who had begun life as a Parisian street artist. His story is told in the documentary film Man on Wire by James Marsh.

Philippe was just 18 when he read an article in his dentist's waiting room about the towers, which had

> Petit believed in his vision so much that he was able to keep his faith and keep going.

not even been built at that point. Nevertheless, he made up his mind that when the towers were built he would walk a high wire between them.

In order to do this walk, he would not only have to have enormous passion and tenacity, but also be incredibly resourceful. Petit planned for six years. He and his friends

made several trips to the towers to collect information, then broke into the towers, hid themselves and their equipment over 100 floors up and rigged a steel cable across the huge 43-m (140-ft) divide. That was all before Petit walked across the wire, buffeted by the winds swaying the cable.

On 7 August, in the early morning, Petit stepped out on to the wire. He walked above Manhattan for 45 minutes, back and forth across the cable. He even lay down for a while. He eventually stopped when the police arrived. They arrested him, but Petit had achieved what he had set out to do all those years before. His incredible feat made headlines all over the world.

What makes this such an inspiring story for me is the fact that Petit believed in his vision so much that he was able to keep his faith and keep going, despite many difficulties and obstacles along the way.

Whatever you want to create in your life you can do it, too, if you know what you want and why. You can hold the picture of what you want in your mind and focus on it, no matter what the odds.

Create a vision for your future

The Twin Towers weren't even built when Philippe Petit first committed to his goal to walk a high wire between them, yet he kept an absolute unwavering belief in his ability to bring about this immense achievement in his life. No one told

> Allow yourself permission to dream about how your future could be.

him he could do this. The belief came from inside him. Do you want your loving future as much as Petit wanted to walk between the Twin Towers? Do you have a picture of what you want to create in your life?

Allow yourself permission to dream about how your future could be. It is not enough just to tell the universe that you want to have love in your life. You need to actively imagine what this will look and feel like when you have it. The spiritual universe responds to the picture of what you want and does its best to bring it towards you as you take real actions to make it happen at the same time. Manifestation comes about as a result of co-creation between you and the spiritual universe.

Treasure maps

When you want to bring something new into your life, it is really useful to create physical images of what you want to manifest.

When you see an image every day it reminds you to focus on what you want. It stimulates and feeds your unconscious in a very easy, light way with pictures of your dreams, helping you to create the energy that magnetizes your new happy future towards you.

The idea of treasure maps came originally from the author Shakti Gawain in the 1970s and her writings on creative visualization. Some people now refer to treasure maps as vision boards, visual prayers or universe wish lists. A treasure map is a collection of personally inspiring images, which together form a picture of what your future will be like when your goals are fully realized. Having that treasure map up on your wall will help to draw in the life represented by those images. Your unconscious just loves visual images that provoke an emotional response.

Create your love treasure map

* Get hold of a pinboard or a large piece of card and start to collect images that represent your new future. In this case you are going to devote your treasure map to images of a new loving future. Just beginning the process of collecting these images can be really motivational and illuminating.

* Start looking for happy pictures. Look through magazines and on the internet, find postcards and photos that represent your dreamed new reality. You are looking for any image that will inspire or motivate you to create this new future and bring it to life.

* When you have chosen your images, get your glue and scissors and make a collage on your board – just like you did at primary school, but this time with more purpose. The rule of thumb is to do it with joy and abundance. What you feed in energetically to your picture is going to make an impact.

* You can also draw the images yourself if that adds even more meaning to your love treasure map. It doesn't matter if you aren't Rembrandt. If a childlike drawing of a house with a family in front of it and a bright-yellow sun in the sky brings you great feelings of happiness, it might be more effective than a perfect photograph from a magazine. The Law of Attraction works on the feelings you attach to an image. The more you can believe that your future is possible and probable, the more of it will be attracted to you.

The images to include

Make sure you include images on your love treasure map that reflect the sort of person you will be when you have attracted love. Think about what your life will be like after you have already achieved this desired future. This will make your unconscious see your future goals not as something you want, but as something that is a foregone conclusion. As soon as this happens, the Law of Attraction can start working its magic and begin to make these pictures a reality.

Perhaps you want pictures of happy friends and family gatherings or of couples holding hands. Think about the life experiences you will have with friends and your loving partner when you have attracted this new life to you. Perhaps you want pictures of a couple travelling together, or having a child together, or a loving couple growing old together? Or a couple getting married, if that's what you want.

Be expansive in your thinking. Remember this is the blueprint that the Law of Attraction will use for your future.

Create a well-rounded life. You could just stick up pictures of people who look like your ideal man/woman, but then what are you going to do with this person when they arrive in your life? What sort of life do you want to have with

them? How do you want to be treated by them? What kind of life values will you share?

Personally I always make sure I have happy scenes of activities I want to pull into my life to create a light, happy, rich life with my friends and partner. You might want to have pictures of dancing, being with animals, spending times in a beautiful place. One picture I have always liked on my treasure map is

> Your unconscious will see your future goals not as a want, but as a foregone conclusion.

an image I found in a travel magazine of a couple climbing up a hiking trail together. They look happy, fit, loving and healthy and they are in a beautiful place. I create a future with travel, love and well being all in one hit!

You'll find you get quite choosy when you start collecting your pictures. You may start with a big pile of pictures and, the more you look at them and get a feel for them, the more you will start to discriminate between those that really resonate with you and those that are just 'so-so'. The guideline? When in doubt chuck them out. Choose only images that are truly nurturing for your soul.

Colour is good; black and white isn't as stimulating to the unconscious as colour. Create a big, bold, bright dream future through your images if you want to create a big, bold future in your reality.

The finished map

Where are you going to put your treasure map? I put mine somewhere I can catch sight of it every day on a wall near where I work. But you could also choose to place it near your love altar (see page 86), in the bedroom as a reminder to bring love in each

> Take delight in your treasure map each day.

morning or even in the corner of your house associated with love from a feng shui point of view. You can even carry a mini collage in your purse or in the front of a notebook you use regularly.

This is a dynamic process. You don't have to keep the images you started with just because they are stuck on the board. Get rid of any picture as soon as it stops inspiring you. Change your pictures, update them. Take delight in your treasure map each day. It was the author

William W. Purkey who first said: 'You've gotta dance like there's nobody watching... Sing like there's nobody listening' and it is a great sentiment. I want your pictures to dance and sing so that they dance and sing to your soul and that vibration goes out to the universe and attracts in love from everywhere. In summary:

* Make your future visual: use pictures not words.

* Choose images that are meaningful to you and make you feel good.

* Keep it private so that you aren't influenced by other people's ideas about what's right for you.

By the way, the results can be immediate. I put a picture of a holiday I wanted to create on my life treasure map and manifested it that very day when a friend invited me away!

Your love list

Spend as long as you like thinking about what you want to create in your life. As well as your love treasure map, keep an ongoing love list of what you want in the love area of your life. A love list is your definition of what love is for you.

What do you want?

A love list starts by clarifying what you want in your life.

What do you really enjoy doing with your life? What kind of activities will give you the feeling of having love in your life? What kind of relationships would you have? What kind of people would be present?

Write down what your life will be like when it is full of love. Imagine and describe in words every area of your life, not just romantic relationships. How will your life change when you have become this new loving person who finds it so easy to attract love? Picasso said: 'Every child is an artist. The problem is how to remain an artist after he grows up.' Be imaginative. Be creative. Indulge yourself. Write down what you really want. Make sure that you don't in any way write down what you think other people would want you to have. Censorship kills dreams. Be as imaginative as you were as a child.

Once you start writing you'll find that you can write really expansively. Check your feelings as you go along. If there is even a tiny part of you that says I am not sure I want this bit, then cut it out and start again.

Remember that when we do something for the very first time it doesn't necessarily feel totally easy

or natural because, of course, it is the very first time. Once you have let yourself get into the swing of this new habit of thinking about a happy, loving future it will become natural. You'll soon discover all these wonderful dreams you have for the future. Let your mind wander naturally.

Explore each picture in turn. Make little adjustments and alterations.

It is important to play, not work at this. Personally I find I do this best by jotting down ideas in a special book I have bought for my love list. Then I can decant the best ideas on to a wall chart so that I have them near me at all times.

Don't force yourself. You will be most creative when you are comfortable, lying in the sun or in a hot bath, meditating or as you wake up in the morning. Just relax and let the ideas come naturally.

Why do you want this?

Look at what you have written in your love list. Then next to each idea for your future write down some reasons why this is so important for you to have in your life. If you decide that it is a 'nice to have' rather than a 'must', then I would suggest that you question whether you really feel passionate enough about it to manifest it in your life. Think about what having this in your life will add to your life. What positive feelings will it bring you? Being clear on why you want a what will really get the good feelings attached to your future dreams.

Read through your love list. Make it as personal as possible. Then really feel that dream coming alive. If you are imagining being with your new love, imagine what your friends will say to you and about you, imagine what loving words you and your partner will exchange. Where will you eat and sleep? What kinds of activities will you do together? What will your life be like on a daily basis? How will you demonstrate your love to each other? Will you travel? Will you write each other love notes? Will you give each other little gifts? What is the most meaningful way someone can demonstrate love to you?

Dream that it is happening and, most importantly, feel it. Remember the more you charge your dreams with emotion and feeling, the more you activate the Law of Attraction.

Harnessing the power of feelings

One thing people don't always understand about the Law of Attraction is that it works on feeling. A client says something like: 'Well, I wrote out my goals, but nothing happened.' So I ask: 'What

do you feel when you imagine achieving your goals?'

I might get an answer like 'not much' or 'I really want these things to happen in my life, but I don't know how to make them happen.'

If I probe a little more, they might say something like: 'I don't feel I can really make that sort of thing happen to me.'

> **The more you charge your dreams with emotion and feeling, the more you activate the Law of Attraction.**

The key word here is 'feel'. If you think you want one kind of life, but feel you will get or deserve another kind, guess which the Law of Attraction will bring you? The Law of Attraction is magnetic. Emotion carries a higher charge of energy than logical, conscious thought.

Every time you think about your past or your future you have an emotion attached to the image in your mind. To demonstrate this, think about the following questions:

* Do you remember what freshly cooked bread tastes like?

* How about the smell of freshly laundered sheets?

* Remember a time when you felt really good about something or someone?

* Do you have a memory of a favourite piece of music?

Recalling pictures or smells or tastes brings up feelings. Although those memories happened in the past, the feelings attached can be brought into the present.

You can make the future happen by putting memories into the future, too. By visualizing what you want in lots of detail, imagining what it will feel like when you are living that future dream, your unconscious starts to believe that it is real. The energy of this future 'memory' acts as a magnet, pulling your new future into your life. The trick is making sure you feel joyful. The

> Once you feel loved and love yourself, you will attract loving experiences and loving people.

stronger your feelings, the easier you will find it to attract what you want.

This is also why it is so vital to spend time on your feelings of loving yourself first before you start creating a new future — otherwise you will just attract what you have always attracted. Negative emotion is a very powerful thing. If you are full of anger you will attract angry people and experiences that bring more anger into your life. If you are full of sadness or unresolved grief from lost love or bad childhood experiences, then you are going to keep creating more loss and sadness in your life through the Law of Attraction. It is therefore enormously important to identify any unresolved negative emotions and to resolve them, as they act as big energy blocks in your unconscious, magnetizing experiences towards you.

Once you have dealt with negative emotions you create an energy gap within your unconscious. Because the highest energy in the universe is love, this will flow into the spaces you have created. Once you feel loved and love yourself, you will attract loving experiences and loving people into your life.

When you think of that new life, what does it feel like? Does it make you feel happy or excited thinking about it? Or do you not have many feelings about it?

If you can't get excited thinking about your future, then you need to change something in the pictures you are making.

Turning your dreams into intentions

If feeling is the first key to success with the Law of Attraction, the second key to success is to make a decision that you will make these dreams happen. As soon as you have made this decision you can turn your 'wants' to 'whens' by creating a series of intentions or goal statements.

Creating a clear intention

Imagine, for example, that one of your intentions is to manifest a relationship by the end of the year. The reason you want this is because you would like to have a partner to enjoy being with at Christmas. Longer term, you want to settle down and have a family. The first actions you intend to take towards this goal are to join a dating agency and also take up a new weekly dance class so that you get out and meet more people.

Write down your intention (also known as a cosmic order). For example:

* 'My intention is that I will be with my new loving partner this Christmas.'

Now imagine a specific scene on this exact day — a moment in the future that you can 'freeze-frame' in your mind, like a future memory. Describe this in as much detail as possible and, as you do this, make sure that it evokes strong positive feelings in you. For example:

'It is December 25th. I am sitting at the table in my home next to my romantic partner. I am really loving being with this person. I can smell the food on the table and feel his arm around me. I can hear him saying that he loves me. At this moment I am so happy. I feel so loved. I feel so loving. I feel so alive...'

Describe what you can see, feel and hear in the scene as specifically as possible. Then say to yourself:

'Thank you for this already having happened in the best way for me to create a happy, balanced life, for everyone around me and to the highest good of all concerned.'

Make as many intention statements as you need to fully flesh out your vision of your future.

Turn your 'wants' to 'whens' by creating a series of intentions or goal statements.

Exercise

Follow these rules to create intention statements

* Take pen and paper and write down your intention (this ensures that you commit to it).

* Write your intention in the present tense as if it is happening to you right now. (This way you feel your intention becoming real.) See it, feel it, hear it. Create an emotional connection to it.

* Be specific about what you want.

* Be clear why you want this – your intention must be personally compelling for it to have sufficient energetic 'charge' to manifest.

* Be clear when you want this. (This helps you to focus clearly on what you will create.)

* Be clear that having this in your life will be good for you and everyone else who might be impacted by it.

* Decide what you are going to do to make this happen as a first step (even if the universe may eventually give it to you in another way).

Now play your part

It's not enough just to think about what you want. The inner work always comes first, but you do need to take some action in the real world as well to manifest your future.

Once you've done the work on the inside, cement your belief that it is going to happen by doing some

> Inner work always comes first, but you need to take action in the real world to manifest your future.

work on the outside as well. It doesn't really matter what that action is, as long as in your mind it is taking you towards what you want. As the saying goes, 'The Gods help those who help themselves'. Simply look at your dream and decide a first step to getting it.

Look back at your intention statement. Now write down any step you could take towards this. This shows the universe you have committed to this vision.

For example: 'I will commit to this new future by joining a dating agency or app this month and starting salsa classes in September [describe what you will do as specifically as possible]. This is the

service and energy that I offer to the universe in return for manifesting my new future.'

If you want to get rich and win the lottery, you have to buy a lottery ticket. If you want to get a great job, then start applying for some. If you want to meet someone, start getting out there — take up some new hobbies, join a dating site. It doesn't really matter what you do as long as your intention is to make things happen.

When you manifest your dreams they may come about in indirect ways and not seem on the surface at least to have come as a direct consequence of the action you have taken. But it is because you have taken an action that they manifest.

Do I need to know every step?

Let's clear up an issue that people are often confused about. Taking action does not mean that you need to know every step that will be required to achieve your dream. It is much more important to be really, really clear about what you want, rather than how you think you are going to get it. As long as you put energy into your dream in some way, and keep focusing on what you want, you will get results. The universe makes miracles happen.

Trust the universe

OK, having said all this, here's the part where some people start getting doubts. Manifestation takes trust. You need to trust and let go of how the universe will help you.

Many people who have written to me about their successes and blocks with the Law of Attraction get as far as being clear on what they want and then start doubting. They go back to negative thinking and doubt that they really can achieve their dreams. They don't trust that the power of the universe will sort things out.

What do you do if you are one of these people?

Stay calm. Go back to earlier chapters and consider the following: are you clinging on to some of your old thought patterns? Have you forgiven yourself and others for your past hurts? Don't try to deny negative or questioning thoughts or batter them down.

> Negative thoughts aren't going to go away simply by you pretending that they aren't there.

Avoid mole-bashing

When I catch people trying to suppress what they are really thinking, it reminds me of the Japanese game called *Moguratati* (mole-bashing), which I used to play in games arcades when I lived in Tokyo. There is a board in front of you with lots of holes in it. As an alarm sounds, a mole pops its head out of a hole and you have to bash it down again. You don't know where the mole is going to come up, so you have to keep alert at all times. Then more than one mole sticks its head up. The game gets faster and faster, with more and more moles appearing.

I regard negative thoughts as a bit like moles. If you just hit them on the head they are only going to stick their heads up somewhere else. They aren't going to go away by you pretending they aren't there.

So, stop bashing your thoughts. Just softly observe them. Acknowledge that these thoughts have appeared for a reason. They are just telling you that they are there so that you have the chance to let go of them once and for all.

Once you have acknowledged them, then gently question them. On the next page are a few questions to get started with.

* Is this a useful way for me to think if I want to attract more love into my life?

* Is this a useful way to think if I want to attract all the love I intend to have in my life?

* Is this a useful way to think if I am going to attract every single one of my dreams in the way I have written them down on my love list?

* Is this a useful way to think if I am going to attract every single one of my dreams in the way I have put them on my love treasure map?

* What would be a more trusting way of thinking?

* What would be a more abundant way of thinking?

* What would be a happier way of thinking?

* What way of thinking would help me to achieve what I want?

* What resources do I already have to achieve what I want?

* What other beliefs would it be useful to adopt to attract the life I want?

* What evidence can I find now to support these beliefs in my life?

Above all, be gentle with yourself. Just keep focusing back on what you want, imagining your new life as if it is happening to you right now. The more you fill out that life in your head, the easier it will be to begin to trust it will happen.

Why 'not wanting something' brings it to you

Here's another trap many of us fall into. Instead of spending our time thinking about how to create a particular future that we do want, we spend our time thinking about

> Keep focusing on what you want, imagining your new life as if it is happening right now.

how we are going to avoid all those things we don't want.

If you are not feeling particularly happy or if you have a chequered history with love, then it's an easy trap to fall into. How many times do you catch yourself having the 'don't want' thoughts?

Here is a common one: 'My goal is to make sure I am never alone or single again.'

When you create a negative intention like this, the universe gets a picture from you of a poor, unhappy person and probably gets a burst of strong emotion attached to it as well. The image and thought forms are so strong that the universe receives the image loud and clear. Being a perfectly responsive universe, it does its best to create the intention it has seen and felt for you. The result is that you inadvertently attract more 'being unhappy and lonely' experiences towards you.

When you catch yourself doing a 'don't want', think about how you could turn it into a 'want' statement instead. For example, 'I want to be with a romantic partner by XX date' or 'My goal is to make sure I see friends for dinner twice a week.'

Manifestation boosters

Changing your beliefs is a way of boosting your magnetic power so that you attract love into your life easily. When you change your thoughts, you change your energy vibration. The more positive your vibration, the easier you are going to find it to attract your dreams and make them into your new reality.

There are various other ways you can boost your magnetic power as well. Here are two more that have proved very successful: the laughter method and the 'acting as though something is true' tactic.

Laughter method

This is one of the simplest things you could ever do. The spiritual universe is a very light, happy vibration. When you manifest happiness, you link into the spiritual universe through your thoughts. If you can be light and happy as you think about what you want to magnetize towards you, then you are going to be very successful. All you have to do is be happy. About 30 minutes of concentrated happiness is enough to raise your vibration to the right level.

I would suggest:

* Watching a good laugh-out-loud comedy on TV

* Dancing around to some stupid music

* Playing a silly game with children or as if you were still a child

As soon as you have finished, imagine your future as though it is happening to you right now.

Act as though...

If you act as if something is true, then it often becomes true. Act as though you are lovable and you will find people pick up on the difference in your behaviour. You give off different vibes. Your body language changes. You look happier. You really feel happier. And guess what?

People want to be around you more. You are more fun to be around. The end result is you get more love in your life. Then, because you are

> **The more you do something, the more it becomes a habit and soon it becomes totally unconscious behaviour.**

getting more love in your life, you feel more lovable. You give it out and receive it back. It is a self-nurturing cycle.

Now you may feel first of all that you are acting, but the more you do something, the more it becomes a habit and soon it becomes totally unconscious behaviour. Before too long it doesn't feel like acting at all. In fact it just becomes part of your identity.

Say thank you

Finally, remember to say thank you in advance to the universe for what it is about to bring into your life. We always say thank you because, in one part of the universe, this change has already been created. Expressing gratitude in advance shows the universe that your beliefs are fully trusting in your ability to manifest this change.

Then keep a look out. As long as you keep taking action and focus on what you want, the universe will bring you what you need in order to keep you on the right path.

Summary

What is your vision of your future? How often do you sit down and really think about the kind of life you want to build? We are co-creators of our futures. If you put in the effort and focus, then the universe will help you by bringing you people and opportunities to change your life. Being a co-creator gives you power and responsibility. You can bring more of what you want into your life and at the same time have less of what you don't want. It all begins with forming a clear, fresh vision of your future.

Take the time to really think about the loving life you want now. Keep your eye on what you want rather than the how you are going to get it. Just let go of the how for the time

being. The universe will sort that out for you in good time. The clearer you can be with your vision, the better. How clear are the pictures you have of this life? Can you gather pictures to help you visualize? Bright, colourful pictures are attractive and memorable for the mind.

To help you to refine your vision, ask yourself why you really want this future. Then chuck out anything you don't feel strongly about. Use your emotions as a guide to keep you on track so that you ask for what you truly want.

Forming a clear vision is the first step forward towards what you want.

Then you can begin to take actions, one at a time, to create your vision. You still don't need to be able to see the whole path to the end goal, but actions show the universe that you are committed to creating this new life. With each action, keep focusing on what you want and trust that the universe knows how best to help you to bring about this happy, loving future.

4: Dream Your Future

'All that we see or seem is but a dream
within a dream.'

Edgar Allen Poe

Once you have had a taste of loving yourself and being loved
by another person you will never want to go back into lack
again. Attracting love isn't something you do once and then
forget about. It is about a changed way of living in the world.
New daily habits can help you to continue your 'love state', as
can night-time dreaming.

The Law of Attraction doesn't stop working just because you are
asleep. Indeed in many spiritual traditions this is the best time to
attract a new life as you can bypass your conscious mind and
contact your spiritual helpers, who will help you to change your
life forever.

In this chapter you will learn how to:

* Work with your dreams to explore where you are
  in your life
* Make a dream catcher
* Use daytime dreaming to reinforce your link
  with the spiritual universe
* Meditate

Dream life

Edgar Allan Poe's quotation about seeing a dream within a dream is also the view of many spiritual traditions across the planet. They see everyday life as a form of dream. When you are asleep you are still living your life within the spiritual universe, as it is just the conscious part of you that is asleep. In the physical universe, life is bound by the laws of time and space and matter. In other vibrations of the universe there is no time or space; no now, and no past, present or future. There is only what we call 'internal reality' – the 'you' who is not contained in a physical body.

If life is just a different dream, then isn't it logical that dreams are just a different part of your life? Dreams are what link us to the invisible spiritual universe: the connecting channel, if you will, between this world and the world we can't see but where our non-physical bodies reside. You can actively work with your dreams as a way of helping you to heal blocks and to activate and enhance your love attraction.

Sleep

In ancient spiritual traditions sleep is seen as the basic state out of which we all come. Before we are born into a physical body on this earth we are naturally in a sleep state, without eyes, ears, nose, tongue and touch. In sleep we return once more to this place we came from, to connect again with the invisible world of the spiritual universe.

You sleep for about one-third of your life. For the average person that's over 25 years of your life spent in a non-waking state. Not all of your time asleep is spent dreaming, but researchers reckon that at least ten years of your life is spent inside a sleeping dream.

Working with your dreams

All of us dream. Some of us appear to dream more than others only because we are better at remembering our dreams. If you are not someone who regularly remembers their dreams, don't worry. It is something you can train yourself to do with practice.

Dreams work on two levels. In broad terms the two types of dreams are:

* Objective dreams – a psychic dream about a real event
* Subjective dreams – personal dreams that can give insights into your current thinking and development

Dreams show us, in either symbols or images, what we are focusing on. Dreams talk to us in pictures and images because a picture is a much stronger representation of an idea than a word can ever be. Sometimes the image is very obvious and easy to interpret. Sometimes it doesn't make sense at first.

At the same time dreams provide a direct channel for the spiritual

> Dreams are what link us to the invisible spiritual universe: the connecting channel.

universe to communicate with us. At night, as you sleep, it is as if there is a direct telephone line opened up between your unconscious self and your higher self and the whole invisible universe, without the block of your conscious mind getting in the way. If you are naturally psychic you may receive future knowledge through dreams or trance about events that are going to happen as you access what are called the Akashic records. This is the infinite store of knowledge, like a library, within the spiritual universe where everything about you – your past, present and future – is held.

Your spirit knows that the universe is one of infinite possibilities. Every resource that you will ever need to resolve any issue is available to you. It works with your unconscious at night to bring this to your attention.

Dreams help you to recognize misconceptions you hold about yourself, different facets of yourself along with your fears, hopes and all other emotions.

Creative Dreaming

Creative or lucid dreaming is a way of working with your dreams to explore where you are in your life and to reach out to the wisdom of your guides and your higher self. Shamans practise this type of dreaming, which means dreaming in an intentional way, keeping control of the outcome of the dream. Lucid dreaming is the more commonly used term, but I like 'creative

> Creative dreaming is a way of working with your dreams to reach out to a higher wisdom.

dreaming' because it emphasizes that you can control dreaming and use it creatively at will. In a lucid dream you are aware that you are dreaming even as you experience the dream. As you wake within the dream you can then direct the dream to wherever you want to take it.

You can learn this same skill as a way to work with your dreams for self-knowledge and for clearing negative emotions as you progress along your love-attraction journey.

The Law of Attraction and dreams

The Law of Attraction helps you attract into your life what you are focusing on at all levels of your being, whether you are awake or asleep. As soon as you begin to work with your dreams to attract love, you will be given insights into what is going on in your life, intuition about people you meet and events you experience as well as anything that still needs to be healed or resolved.

By working with your dreams, you will get clues as to what is going on in your unconscious thinking and be able to resolve issues at the deepest levels. At the same time this will help you to practise daily at communicating with your higher self to bring in love every day.

Dreams are sources of great wisdom. By becoming aware of your dream travels each night, you can tap into higher guidance for your waking state every day.

There are two ways to help attract love through dreaming – dream interpreting and the RISC technique.

Method 1: Dream Interpreting

This method uses dreams as a spyhole on to your inner world. Deliberately remembering your dream gives you clues as to what stage you have reached in moving on from past hurts or patterns of attracting love. Dreams can alert you to specific issues that need to be dealt with before you can move on to the next stage. They let you know both the problem and often the solution as well.

Dreams will weave a story out of your everyday experiences and imagination to bring the issue to your attention.

An easy way to begin working with your dreams is to pay attention. One of my spiritual teachers used to tell me: 'If you don't pay attention, you'll pay in other ways' (meaning pain and suffering, I think!). You can also put it another way – pay attention and you'll get a big, positive pay-off as well. As soon as you start to pay attention to your dreams the spiritual universe will then help you by giving you dream messages about how you can overcome the issue and move on with your life.

There are many books on the subject of dream symbol interpretations. Some symbols can be intensely personal in their meanings. Other symbols are 'archetypes' and have universal meanings. For example, if you dream about a house, this is generally taken to be the 'self'. You can look up these universal meanings in dream books, but

> **Dreams will weave a story out of everyday experiences and imagination to bring the issue to your attention.**

do be aware that some symbols will also have unique meanings for you. A particular person in a dream represents a part of your personality that you may or may not be aware of. If there is a dominant character in the dream it is useful to think about the characteristics of that person. How do they mirror aspects of yourself? If you are not certain, it may be because he or she is mirroring something that you are unaware of in yourself. If you are not sure, let the question stay with you until your unconscious gives you some other clues.

It is helpful to spend time thinking about each part of the dream in turn. What does each event or image mean to you? Some dreams point to our fears and some to our desires. What idea do you most associate with the particular image? For example, I associate water with the flow of emotions, so a leaky tap for me is emotions leaking out when I am trying to suppress them. A baby for me symbolizes the part of me that is undeveloped and needs protecting. A fast car is a method of getting somewhere. As well as symbolizing learning, a school symbolizes a place where there are rules and restrictions, but also perhaps safety and security.

Let your personal association with each image come into your mind and, if you are not certain, ask for another dream to clarify whatever you are still not sure about.

Exercise

Set intentions to dream

* Keep a pad of paper and a pen by your bedside at night. Intend before you go to sleep that you will dream about whatever you want to know about. Here are some examples of the sort of intentions you could set:

'I intend to dream about anything that is blocking me from having a happy relationship right now.'
'I intend to dream about how I can overcome this/these blocks.'
'I intend to dream about what actions would be useful for me to take right now that will move my life forward to love, in a way that is to my highest good.'

* Once you have set an intention to dream and remember the relevant parts of the dream, your unconscious will know that you are serious and you are more likely to remember what's important when you wake up in the morning.

* As soon as you awaken, write down as much of the dream as possible. Pay attention to the story, the characters, the setting of the dream, the events and most importantly the feeling you were left with. By recognizing this feeling you will often get the meaning intuitively.

Method 2:
The RISC Technique

As you begin to clear and untangle the old belief habits that have prevented you from attracting love in the past, you may find that you naturally experience vivid dreams. This is a good indicator that you are in the middle of a shift in your life. In your dreams, your higher self and your unconscious will seek to resolve anything that needs resolving. It is good to recognize that, even with a dream that is not entirely comfortable to you, your higher self is showing you what you are ready to resolve.

If you have a dream with negative feelings, you can employ a very effective and now widely used tool developed by Dr Rosalind Cartwright called the RISC Technique. It has four steps to it.

> In your dreams, your higher self and your unconscious will seek to resolve anything that needs resolving.

R = Recognize

Notice when you are having a dream that leaves you feeling negative. For example, you may wake up feeling afraid, tearful or stressed.

I = Identify

Think about the characters and story of the dream. What happened that made you feel uncomfortable? What precisely was emotional or disturbing about the dream?

S = Stop

Once you have practised lucid dreaming (see page 66), it becomes very easy to stop a dream the moment it becomes uncomfortable. As soon as you become aware of the negative feelings, either wake yourself up or change the plot within the dream.

C = Change

You can change the storyline within the dream and you can also transform your thinking about your dream after you awaken. One of the simplest ways to break the dream is to physically turn over. We tend to find it easier to lucid dream lying on our right sides. Turn to your left and the plot line will change anyway. When you wake up, you can imagine where you wanted the dream story to go and rehearse the new ending. For example, if you felt weak or helpless during the dream, make yourself strong in your

Stand up for yourself.
You can change any dream to have an empowering outcome.

actions. Stand up for yourself. You can change any dream to have an empowering outcome.

Practising this technique stops recurring dreams, but most importantly helps you to resolve deep emotional issues.

Love dream catcher

The dream catcher is a psychic protection tool. Of Native American origin, dream catchers are made to hang above the bed and catch bad dreams like a spider catches its prey inside the web. According to legend, the dream catcher ensures that only good dreams enter your mind when you dream at night. It also protects against general negative energies.

Making your own dream catcher, rather than buying one, is far more powerful as it becomes like any other psychic tool or ritual – a repository for your intention to let go of the old stuff in your life and replace it with the new.

Your dream catcher then becomes something you can hang over your bed and see last thing at night and first thing in the morning as a symbol of this new you. I have two dream catchers myself – one made especially for me by hand and strewn with little rose-quartz crystals and one that I made myself, which contains various feathers and stones that have particular meanings for me.

The dream catcher ensured that only good dreams enter your mind.

Make a love dream catcher

Make this for yourself and it can become another tool to attract love into your life through the power of the Law of Attraction.

Either bend a wire coat hanger into a circle or purchase a large metal or wooden ring from a craft shop. This will form the outside of your 'web'.

* Take some ribbon or suede lacing and glue one end to the ring, then wrap the ribbon tightly around and around the ring until it is completely covered. Stick the end of the ribbon down with glue to secure it in place.

* Now take some stiff thread and tie one end to the ring. You are going to make a web of thread across the ring by making half-hitch knots at evenly spaced intervals around the ring. To do this take the thread, loop it over the ring, then bring it back towards you by pulling it through the space between the thread and the ring. Keeping the thread taut between each knot, work around the ring, spacing your knots evenly – about 2.5 cm (1 in) or 5 cm (2 in) apart.

* As you work, you can thread small beads or crystals on to the thread if you like. I suggest clear quartz, turquoise or rose quartz as these are crystals associated with love and protection.

✳

* Once you have finished the outer 'row', work an inner 'row' by placing each knot between the knots of the previous row. Continue making inner rows in this way, working towards the middle of the web, until all you are left with is a tiny hole in the centre. Put a feather or shell in this central point and then tie the thread to secure it, and glue if necessary.

* To complete the dream catcher, attach feather tassels to what will be the 'bottom' of the ring when it is hung up. String feathers and beads on to a piece of thread or suede and secure these to the ring. To finish, make a suede loop for the top, by which to hang it up.

* Now create your intention for the dream catcher. Take some time and sit with it. Make the decision that it will be a tool to help you remove from your life forever the unhelpful energetic thought forms that have prevented you from receiving love in abundance and to your highest good. Intend that it is an instrument to bring you healing in your dreams so that you are open to love and receive all the love available in life, with the help of your higher self and spirit guides.

* Now hang the dream catcher above your bed.

Daytime dreaming

You can take even more control of your love dreams by dreaming during the day as well as at night.

Many spiritual traditions don't just use dreams for answers to life. They also deliberately change one's conscious state to replicate the conditions found in dreaming, thereby accessing the higher levels of the universe beyond the constraints of time and space to find great wisdom and guidance. In ancient cultures such as Babylon, dreams were a way of receiving messages from the gods. Through dreams and changes of conscious state you could foretell the future or understand divine will. In Native American culture shamans alter their states of awareness deliberately to communicate with the subtle energies of spirit animals and guides. Some traditions use natural drugs to produce a trance,

> Open up a clear channel between your unconscious mind and your higher self.

others use drumming to produce ecstatic states, some use different forms of meditation.

All of these have the same effect – to take you out of your normal waking state to a place where your brainwaves slow down, just as they do in sleeping, to either alpha-wave level or the even slower theta-wave level.

As this happens, your vibration changes and you open up a clear channel between your conscious mind and your unconscious mind, as well as between your unconscious mind and your higher self and spirit guides. This allows an easier flow of messages between the higher realms of the spiritual universe and the 'you' sitting here in the material world.

Meditation and trance

I have always thought the word meditation slightly off-putting. When I was younger I used to think it was something really difficult that you had to spend years learning how to do. I got that impression partly from all those pictures of Zen monks sitting cross-legged in silence and partly from the exorbitant prices that some institutions charge for meditation classes.

You don't need to be an amazingly trained or evolved person to meditate or go into a trance. When I trained as a hypnotherapist and started experimenting with self-hypnosis I realized I didn't feel much different in that state than I did when sitting looking out over the famous Ryoanji Zen meditation garden in Japan.

There are many different forms of trance. During the day we all slip

> # When you are meditating your focus changes; you can learn to do this in various ways.

naturally in and out of different states, which are mild trances. When I am driving, for example, I find I reach my destination and realize that I have been driving without really thinking at all about what I was doing. That's a form of trance.

Relaxing deeply while sitting in your favourite chair listening to a beautiful piece of classical music is a form of trance. Daydreaming is trance. That in-between state when you are neither asleep nor fully awake first thing in the morning is a form of trance.

All that 'meditate' means is to 'go to the centre'. When you are meditating your focus changes. You can learn to do this in various ways.

Some people prefer the Eastern form of meditation, where you sit straight-backed on a chair or cross-legged in silence, focusing on only one idea and letting go of other thoughts that drift into your awareness.

Personally, I prefer a more focused trance, called 'active meditation', with a background of sound or music in the shamanistic tradition. In this method, you can either sit or lie down. You can buy guided shamanic healing trances or choose your own piece of gentle classical music to listen to.

When you have learned to relax easily, you can ask to meet your guides to give you messages in your room of relaxation while you are in this trance state. Remember that the messages you receive may well be in the form of symbols or pictures flashing into your mind. When you come out of the meditation let your mind focus softly on what you have received until the meaning of the message comes to your mind.

Learn to meditate

* Set yourself a time limit. I would start with about 15 minutes in total and then progress to a regular 30-minute meditation.

  * Find a place free of any distractions (see page 104) in which to meditate.

* Sit straight-backed in a chair. Your legs should be uncrossed. This is the ideal position for meditation as it opens up the energy channel of the spine, which can act as a conductor, bringing down higher vibration energies from the spiritual universe into this world. Close your eyes and take a big deep breath, then let it out through the mouth. Let your body relax. Let your arms rest gently on your lap, let your legs sink into the floor.

* Set your intention before you close your eyes. What do you want to learn by meditating today? Or do you just want to see what your unconscious reveals in the trance state? Either is fine. Your unconscious will help you to become aware of the answer to specific questions or will throw up images that will help you generally in your personal progress.

* Now take two more deep breaths and exhale through the mouth. As you breathe out, feel any tension just drop out of your body. You can say to yourself: 'As I breathe out, all tensions and worries and stresses of the day melt away into the floor below. I am deeply relaxed.'

＊

* Feel your eyelids become heavy. If you wish, you can check your eyelids. Slowly open them and close them, feeling the relief of being able to close them again, and go further into deep relaxation – this wonderful state of daytime dreaming meditation.

* Now imagine that there is an elevator in front of you. You walk into the elevator and see that there are ten floors. You are currently on the tenth floor and you can press the button with '1' on it so that you can go all the way down. As the elevator descends, each button lights up in turn so that you can see the numbers flashing down, 10, 9, 8, 7, 6, 5, 4, 3, 2, 1.

* When you reach the first floor you will see the door to a room in front of you. This is your room of relaxation. There is a bed here. It looks so comfortable. Enter the room and lie down and totally relax.

* Remain in this place for five minutes or so at first (extend the time as you become more practised).

* When you want to come out, just get back into the elevator and press the button to the tenth floor. See the numbers going up from one to ten. When you reach the ninth floor, feel the energy beginning to return to your body. As you reach the tenth floor take a big deep breath. Open your eyes and slowly bring yourself up to conscious awareness, feeling the energy return to your legs and arms and eyes and mouth and head and neck. Feel your breathing come back to normal. Wake up easily and when you are ready you can get up.

Summary

At night your conscious mind can step out of the way and your powerful link to the spiritual universe is revealed. You are used to dreaming. You may not have ever thought of using your dreams to help you to find love. Start to become aware of the dreams you have at night-time. The spiritual universe sends you messages in your dreams to help you with your personal development and everyday life.

If you want to ask for help around a particular area of your life — find out if you have a block or how to get over a block — you can practise lucid dreaming.

Deliberately use dreams creatively to discover more about your progress to love. Meditation is a form of daytime dreaming which also links you to the spiritual universe and provides you with its wisdom. You can interpret the symbols you see in your meditation in the same way as those in your dreams.

Meditation will also help you to become sensitive to other energies within the spiritual universe and will reinforce any of the exercises you do in the next two chapters.

5: Love Rituals

'The miracle is not to fly in the air, or
walk on the water, but to walk on
earth.'

Chinese Proverb

This chapter describes some simple love rituals you can carry
out. Spiritual rituals and ceremonies are a way of connecting to
the sacred and divine universe. They are used by many spiritual
traditions as a way of reinforcing the belief that what you want
to manifest will actually happen.

When you carry out a ritual you are acting out symbolically your
new, intended future. You show the universe the experience you
would like to bring about in your own life by focusing your
attention on a symbol of that new life. Performing the ritual in a
measured and focused way helps to reinforce the energy of
the intention.

In this chapter you will learn how to:

* Create a home environment to attract love

* Create your own love altar

* Use the power of plants, scents and crystals
  to attract love

Creating a loving home

Your home can become a powerful symbol and living ritual to love. Over the last ten years or so sacred geomancy (a method of divination) and feng shui have become much better known in the West. We now understand what the Chinese and other cultures have known for hundreds of years – that the arrangement of our physical space can impact upon our lives.

I lived in the Far East for a number of years and in one of the offices where I worked one of my wealthiest colleagues had paid her feng shui advisor to look at the layout of the office and advise where she should best place her desk to make money. I remember being quite sceptical at the time, but I gradually learned to take feng shui seriously as she made millions! A turning point for me was when I moved into an apartment and discovered that both my love and wealth corners were missing. Six months after moving in I had resigned my very well-paid job and split up from my boyfriend. A friend who was trained in space-clearing took a look at my home and said it needed urgent work. She spent several hours carrying out energetic clearing in the home. The strangest thing happened immediately afterwards. I came home and found a pool of water in the middle of the

floor. An old, disconnected pipe in the ceiling, probably over 50 years old, had released the water it was carrying as soon as the energetic clearing had happened. It has often been my experience since that water leaks happen in my home when old stagnant energies are being released. Within a month of the space-clearing I had a new job and a few months later a new relationship.

However much you do or don't want to delve into this subject, I think most of us would at least admit that the space in which we live and work can have a big effect on our mood and general emotions. The home is a powerful mirror of the self.

The energy of a home

When you look around your home, what do you feel? Is it full of things you love to see? Does it lift up your energy when you walk in at night or wake up in the morning, or drag your energy down? Do you feel it is a calm and healing space for you?

A home is an outer representation of what is going on for you inside.

You may not be rich enough to have the biggest home or fill it with the most expensive things, but you can still create a loving and nurturing space. This is a very important step towards loving yourself. People who love themselves and attract love create loving environments. Their homes are filled with objects that overflow with loving energy.

You may have had the experience of going into someone's house to feed an animal or water the plants while they are away. Have you ever noticed how even when you walk into an empty house you can still feel the energy or atmosphere connected with the people who live there? It is sometimes so strong that I feel intrusive just by being there. In fact, it is a fairly common experience to feel like whispering or walking around quietly in case you disturb something, even if no one is

> ## The space in which we live and work can have a big effect on our mood and emotions.

actually there! That's because you unconsciously pick up on energies even if you are unaware of them or haven't been trained in any energy work.

Energy can be even stronger in a home where someone is present. Think about two different situations you may have been exposed to in the past. First, have you ever walked into a home where someone is ill or very depressed? What did you feel?

Did you want to hang around or was it an uncomfortable experience? You probably didn't feel entirely at ease because the energy would have been low and would have started to bring down your own energy unless you knew how to protect yourself.

In contrast, have you ever walked into a warm, loving family house where you knew the inhabitants were happy and content? I bet you wanted to hang around in that energy. Most of us would because the love energy would be nurturing for anyone who walked in there.

Start to look around your own home and become attuned to the atmosphere. Is it a peaceful place? A happy place? A loving place?

You are in this space regularly, if not every day. If it is not feeding you and reflecting back to you the loving energy that you want in your life, then it's time to change things. It was the designer William Morris who said: 'Have nothing in your house that you do not know to be useful or believe to be beautiful.'

I believe we should only own objects that are beautiful or loved. You should feel good when you wake up in the morning and look around. Even if you are not consciously noticing all the things in your home, unconsciously you are doing so.

To make your home ready for your new life, look at everything in there.

How would you read your home if you were walking into it for the first time? Remember to pay attention to the garden as well because this is part of your home space.

Have a clear-out

There are a few very basic things you can do as a way of honouring yourself and your wish to attract new energies and love into your home.

First, start by clearing clutter to get rid of old stagnant energy. It's time to ditch all the useless stuff. Get rid of anything associated with bad times or bad relationships. Get rid, too, of anything associated with a past identity. If you have clothes that make you feel frumpy or unattractive, it doesn't matter how useful they are, chuck them out.

Most of us have too many things. Everything you own is connected to you by an energetic cord connection. How much stuff are you connected to? Think about how much energy that is consuming. If you never have space in your home, how can you have space in your head? We tend to hold on to things because we have a lot vested in them. Sometimes it is about lack. For example, I had better keep that in case I can't afford another one. Let

go of your physical bits and pieces and you will find you'll let go of a whole load of mental clutter as well.

Pay attention to the things you own

Often, someone who is single has pictures of single people on their walls. Instead, and in order to attract love, hang up pictures of happy times with friends and happy couples.

All the material possessions you are carrying around you are part of your past and present identity. Think about what you want to carry forward into the next phase of your life. Do you really need that broken piece of China, or the pair of trousers you liked two years ago, or the vase your aunt gave you as a present?

Consider how much freer you will feel with gaps where these things used to be and with space in your life. Imagine what it will be like when you have your new love in your life, or those new friends round for dinner, or your lovely family Christmas in your new happy, loving life. Do you have a table ready for them to eat off? Do you have space in your wardrobe for your new love to hang his or her clothes? Is there room to let people into your home? If there isn't, clear a space.

The rule of the universe is: create a space in your life and the universe will fill it in, so create space with the belief that you will manifest the love you want in the way you want.

Clean the energy of your home

It is important to cleanse the energy of your home from time to time, especially when you have been moving stuff around, by which I mean both material possessions and emotional energy. You should also clean spaces when you move somewhere new or when there has been illness around. Physically clean the room and open windows to let in fresh air.

If you have the money and want to do a more dramatic clearing, then paint your home or even re-carpet. The more you do, the more you will change the effects on your life. Make sure your windows are clean, too, as these relate to your eyes, so dirty windows mean you are not seeing clearly. When the room is physically clean, you can clean its energy.

I always clean the energy of a room before I do a major visualization or meditation as well. It is simply a way of raising the vibration of the space and achieving a clear channel through which to magnetize love or whatever you want to manifest

towards you. You don't need to be trained to do space-clearing. We humans are sensory creatures. You can use sound, smell and light to change the vibration of a space. You can also use breath or simply the power of thought. Take a look around your home and think loving thoughts about it. Project love with your mind into every room. This will begin to raise the vibration of your home.

To raise your home's vibration, first of all think about the lighting there.

It should feel welcoming and warm. Lighting candles is a lovely way to change the energy of a room.

Music is a very quick way to change the vibration of a space, which is why it is used in every sacred tradition. Every type of music has an effect on vibration. You'll need to experiment, but personally I find classical, especially violin, music to be very effective in space-clearing. Japanese and shamanic drumming can bring a very quick change in vibration if you are going to do a ritual within a room. Pop music can bring in a happy or fun vibration that can be very welcoming, but be careful of any music with negative, unloving lyrics. Remember every thought affects the vibration around you. Fill your home with loving lyrics!

Perform the 'love my home' ritual

Here is an intentional ritual you can do to clear your home as part of your love-attraction strategy:

* Start by washing your hands. Take off your shoes and jewellery. Light a white candle and burn some incense.

  * Now sit quietly for a while and just breathe. Appreciate the space you are in. Notice the energy of your home. Set your thought intention that by cleansing your space today you will bring your new loving life into your home. Be aware of how powerful just this thought is.

  * You are going to 'smudge' your space, an idea that comes from Native American tradition, – using a smudge stick. These are made of dried herbs, commonly sage (burning sage is very powerful), and widely available from mind-body-spirit shops and via the internet. Light a smudge stick to clean old energy out of each room.

* Blow out the stick so that smoke comes out of it. Walk around your home and make sure the smoke wafts into every corner clearing out the old energy. As you walk around, state your intention to blow out the old energy and let in the new.

✳

* Clap in each corner of each room low down, in the middle and high up to shift the energy. You can also chant a mantra if you know one, for example the Green Tara goddess mantra (see page 104), or just state your intention loudly to the house.

* Bells are used traditionally in many places as a way of getting rid of negative spirits. Ring the bell in the centre of the room and in each corner of the room to lift the energy after you have clapped. (If you have one, a traditional musical instrument from Asia called a singing bowl works very well instead of a bell.)

* After you have cleaned the energy, wash your hands again. You can now use clean water to anoint the freshly cleansed corners of the rooms. At the same time visualize light coming into the room like a shield all along the outside walls of your home to keep this loving new energy inside. You can also visualize this light as spiralling all around the house.

* Finish the ritual by cleansing yourself. Take a bath with sea salt or Epsom salts to disperse any negative energy you have picked up.

Bedroom

Pay particular attention to the bedroom if you want a new relationship. If you have a bed that is associated with a past love, ideally you want to change the mattress, but if you can't afford to, then smudge all around the bed.

It is also good to have matching bedside tables so that when you and your partner share a bed your power is balanced. In fact, twos of things generally are good in this room.

In Chinese feng shui, red is a good colour to have in the bedroom. Think about putting a red cushion on your bed or perhaps a picture with some red in it.

Plants can raise the energy anywhere in the home and they are great to have in the bedroom. A big plant is better than a small one. You can also experiment with a traditional way to bring romance into the room, which is to keep a vase with red or pink flowers on your bedside table. Make sure the flowers are kept fresh to keep the energy in the room raised. Not all feng shui traditions believe in having plants in the bedroom, by the way, so you may find opinions on this vary.

Creating a love altar

Another powerful ritual you can carry out in your new cleansed space is to set up a love altar. Choose a place where you can create a small sacred space which you can honour and pay attention to on a daily basis. On your altar keep pictures or objects linked with what you want to manifest. You may want to display pictures of you as a happy person, or of couples. Perhaps a symbol associated with a wedding?

Crystals have powerful vibrations, so do place them on your altar. You can put flower offerings (see page 90) or fresh vases of flowers there and burn incense or candles to provide positive energy. You can also offer food or fruit to the energy of the altar.

Open up the power of your altar

Flow energy each day to your altar by holding your left (receiving) hand up to the universe to receive divine light and your right (giving) hand down to the altar. Clear your mind as you do this and hold only the intention of what you intend to bring into your life.

If you keep an altar it's important to keep it fresh and not let it go stale. If you feel that you can't keep up your altar at any point, then rather than neglect it, take it down consciously with thanks for all it has brought into your life so far. You can burn natural oils to scent your altar, choosing one that is particularly appropriate for you, for example to overcome a fear of loving or of being unloved (see below).

Essential oils for your love altar

Property	Suggested oils
Overcome fear of loving	Neroli, ylang ylang or carnation
Overcome fear of being unloved	Rose otto
Overcome fear of change	Frankincense, ylang ylang or lavender
Release fear of emotions	Sandalwood, neroli or frankincense
Antidotes to loneliness	Roman camomile or bergamot
Release doubt	Basil, coriander or ylang ylang
Counteract past abuse thought forms	Rose otto, Roman camomile, mandarin or neroli
Heal the hurt inner child	Neroli, geranium or rose otto
Promote happiness and joy	Rose, orange, jasmine, geranium, clove, ginger or benzoin
Boost self-esteem	Sandalwood, carnation, jasmine, geranium, cedarwood, rose maroc or ylang ylang
Increase self-awareness	Clary sage, pine, bay, mandarin, coriander or jasmine
Connect to divine joy, for burning	Frankincense before meditations for manifesting

Exercise

Create clay love figures

The more personal your symbols, the more powerful they are. This is an example of a ritual you can do around your altar specifically for a love relationship:

* Take clay or moulding clay and make two figures – one to represent you and one your love who will soon manifest in your life. As you make them, intentionally endow them with all the qualities you want to manifest in their lives as they come together. Again, intention is everything. Think about the loving person you are and the loving person you are bringing to you.

* When you complete your figures, join them together in some way to symbolize the powerful energetic joining that will soon be happening. You can put the hands together or tie them together loosely with a single red ribbon. The loose binding signifies your intention to bring your love in, with permission from his or her higher self for the higher good of both of you.

* Place the figures on your altar and see your love as already manifest in your life.

* Remember, always do rituals with the intention that the best outcome for your life as a whole is manifest. Never force anything and certainly never try to force a particular person to come towards you. That is playing with your karma and will not have a good outcome for you.

The power of plants

Flowers and plants look and smell beautiful and have therefore been used in many parts of the world as both love potions and in spiritual ceremonies. Visit a Buddhist temple and you will be overwhelmed by the scent of incense, and also see many vibrantly coloured offerings in the form of fruit and food. In Catholic or Orthodox Christian churches notice how scent is used to raise the energy of the space.

In ancient forms of divination natural fragrant substances like

> By choosing particular plants, you can help your own energy.

frankincense are used to prepare the diviner to enter a trance so they can access the higher levels of the universe and draw on the wisdom of their spiritual helpers. In Indian tantrism, too, smells are used as a preparation for ritual.

In Chinese tradition, the energy, or *qi* (*ch'i*) of a plant and of the place where something is grown can vary. By choosing particular plants or by choosing a plant from a beautiful location, you can help your own energy. At the most basic level, think how your mood is lifted when you are surrounded by flowers or

when you are sitting by a beautiful river. This is because of the energy from the flowers or place. This principle can be used for healing.

The power of the energy of place or nature can be demonstrated in a non-spiritual way. If you sit outdoors in a beautiful green space, scientists know that your cortisol and stress levels are likely to fall as the sights and smells and energy of the space affect you. Similarly, recent studies show that having flowers on the breakfast table to greet you in the morning makes you feel happier for the rest of the day.

In spiritual traditions the effect is more than just stress relief. The *qi* (*ch'i*) of the beauty and scent of nature can be drawn on as a way of attracting love into our lives. Love is a beautiful, joyful, light vibration. To attract it, feed your visual and olfactory senses with beauty and joy and you will attract more love into your life.

The Pusanga

Pusangas come from the Peruvian spiritual tradition. They are scented flower potions, which are used as tools to attract whatever you want into your life and are often used as love magic.

In the Amazon, *pusangas* are made from the highest *qi* (*ch'i*) plants and from water gathered from sacred or magical places. Plants are chosen for their flowers, shapes, scents and colour and laid out together. Scented liquids are often added to make them highly fragrant. When the *pusangas* is ready it is empowered by the shaman. He blows the intention, for example 'health, wealth and love', into the *pusangas*, sometimes simply using his breath and sometimes using tobacco smoke, which is seen as sacred.

If you wish to make a *pusanga*, you can follow the same principles (see page 91). First gather up some beautiful flowers. You don't need to pick the whole stem, just the flower heads will be enough. It is better to pick your own flowers though, so you can choose that they come from a place of significance.

Certain flowers carry specific meanings in many spiritual traditions (see opposite). They may also carry personal meanings for you. If you can, choose ones that have some relationship to what you want to manifest. If roses mean love to you, for example, include roses. Pay attention to the colours of the flowers and their scents. Again, colour is a very powerful vibration. Thank the flowers as you pick them for the energy, they are bringing to you.

Flowers and their meanings

Begonia: Bringing balance into your life

Bougainvillea: Emotional protection and surrender to trust the higher power

Chinese lavender: Transformation

Gardenia: A mirror that doesn't deceive or distort

Hibiscus: Happiness and quiet power

Lily: Purity

Lotus: The divine

Marigold: Readiness for change

Mignonette: Making life beautiful

Myrtle: Overcoming everyday difficulties

Narcissus: Bringing together beauty and the divine

Nasturtium: Encouragement in difficult times

Pink gladioli: Opening up your emotions so you are willing to receive good things in your life

Poinsettia: Surrendering the ego and being open

Rose: Open heart

Snapdragon: Increasing your power to manifest

Ylang ylang: Clearing your mind of illusion

Create a pusanga

* First, cleanse your space using incense or aromatherapy oils to create a beautiful environment.

* Lay a cloth out on the floor and arrange your flowers or plants to look beautiful. You could lay them out in a pattern to look like a Buddhist mandala (a sacred circular design that symbolizes the universe).

* Add other pretty objects at this point if you like. Glitter or fake jewels are all pretty, so will produce good energy.

* Scent the *pusanga* with aromatherapy oils or a natural scent like orange flower water.

* Now set your intention. Breathe into the *pusanga* your clear intention to manifest a new sparkling future, as beautiful as the *pusanga* in front of you.

* To use the *pusanga* as a scent, add spring water to it and bottle it. Use the liquid to anoint or scent your wrists and neck with your manifestation intention. You might also wish to lay it on your love altar (see page 86), or you could take your *pusanga* to a place that is special to you and leave it as an offering.

Give back to the earth to receive love

You might like to make an offering of your *pusanga* in a special place. In Peruvian shamanism, offerings, or *offerenda* in Spanish, are given to the earth as a thank you for bringing in positive things into one's life. In the past I have made offerings like this to a very old tree, which carries the energy of hundreds of years of

Make an offering in a special place.

natural wisdom. In ancient wisdom certain places in nature carry a higher energetic charge – the Chinese would call it a higher vibration of *qi* (*ch'i*). By connecting with these places we can take on this energy and raise our own vibrations and our ability to manifest. Why not find your own special place in nature which carries a positive charge for you and make regular offerings there? By doing so you will raise the energy connected with your intention still further. Each time you connect with this place in thought or meditation you then connect with a strong spiritual vibration and raise your own energy, helping you to attract all that you want into your life.

Using crystal power to attract love

A crystal is an object with a specific vibration that acts as a powerful transmitter of energy to and from the universe. Crystals have been used for many years for healing and magical work.

You can also use crystals for love-attraction programming. I suggest that you use either a clear quartz or rose quartz. The rose quartz is the classic crystal of the heart and healing. Simply wearing a rose-quartz necklace or ring, or having it in your home or by your bedside, helps to bring in the vibration of love because that is the vibration the crystal is most tuned into.

To programme the crystal, all you need to do is direct your focus to the crystal. As in every ritual you carry out, your intention is key. Decide what you want to manifest and get a clear picture of it in your mind.

Cleaning your crystal

First, make sure you have a clean crystal – I mean energetically clean, of course. Don't assume that because you have bought a new crystal from a shop that its energy is clean. When I walk around a crystal shop and hold many of the crystals, I am amazed at the murkiness of the energy of so many of them. It's because they have absorbed the energy of either the location or all the people handling them. Think how you feel after your daily commute and you will understand why your poor crystal needs cleaning. You can leave the crystal outside in the sun and moonlight, partly buried in earth but with the tip sticking out, for three days to clean it. You can also wash the crystal in water and rock salt and, as you do this, imagine the top of your head opening up as you channel universal white light and love down into the crystal, taking away any negative energy.

Honour and respect your own instinct above others.

If you are sensitive you will feel the difference in the energy after cleaning it when you hold it on the palm of your hand. I personally have always felt this as a tingling feeling. Other people feel warmth or cold or just have a sensation of lightness. You will become more attuned to different energies the more you use crystals. Of course if you instinctively don't like the look or feel of a crystal, don't use it. There will be one that is right for you and you should always honour and respect your own instinct above others, since trusting your own

power and knowledge is part of the process of learning to love and honour yourself.

Crystal love-attraction programming

This ritual follows exactly the same principles as every other ritual you have carried out. The key is to get a picture with feelings attached to it. See yourself on your wedding day, joyfully happy and laughing with friends and family.

Now take that picture in your mind's eye and transfer it into the crystal. Set the crystal on your love altar (see page 86) or another special place. You can also wear the programmed crystal. The crystal will transmit your image to the universe, rather like a beacon flashing out light on a dark night lets people from miles around know where something is. The energies of the programmed crystal beam out to the invisible universe, pulling in the future you have programmed. The more the original image you have programmed in resonates with you, the stronger the force of the crystal.

If your dream partner is taking time to show up, a crystal grid (see page 95) will radiate more power than a single crystal. Place your crystal grid on your love altar or other special place in the home where it won't be interfered with.

Other love crystals

Diamonds

Although we associate diamonds with engagement rings and therefore marriage, diamonds aren't as love-attracting as rose quartz. They attract fidelity, long life and sexuality instead.

Emeralds

Emeralds are love amplifiers. However, they stimulate love to all things on earth rather than specifically romantic love. If you want to increase your general feelings of love, then wear an emerald ring or pendant. A pendant that rests over the heart chakra (see page 43) will act like a battery, charging the forces of love around you and bringing love into your life from all directions.

Jade

This is the stone of the Chinese Goddess of Love and Compassion, Guan Yin (see page 101). It is a healing stone, which also attracts romance and love to you. In addition, this powerful gem attracts prosperity, so if you wear it you will magnetize abundance into your life in many ways.

Black obsidian

This gemstone is protective. If you pick up other people's energies too readily and get knocked back by negative atmospheres, then wear this close to your heart so that the energies are deflected from your aura, and you receive only the loving energies around you.

Make a crystal love grid

* You need eight clear crystals or a mix of crystals and rose quartz. Many crystal shops sell small inexpensive crystals as smooth round stones called 'tumbled stones', which are fine for this purpose. Make sure they are clean.

* Select one of the eight crystals to be your 'charging crystal'. Now arrange six of the crystals in a circle with their tips pointing inwards. Place the seventh in the centre. If it has a point, this can point in any direction towards the other stones, but not upwards.

* Now set your intention. Ask that your highest spiritual guides, higher self and universal love purify and charge this grid to bring love into your life in a way that is in accordance with your highest good. You can also use this grid to bring in general healing of any issues in your life in accordance with your highest good. If you have any angels who are special to you, ask for their energies as well at this point.

* Take your charging crystal in your right hand and imagine channelling this loving, healing energy into each crystal on your grid, flowing the energy through your charging crystal, pointed to each crystal in turn as if the charging crystal is a magic wand.

* Finally connect up the grid. Flow the energy through your charging crystal to the centre crystal, then to one of the outer crystals, on to the next crystal and back to the centre so that you make a series of pie segments. Move counterclockwise around the grid until you close the circle. As you do this, keep your intention clear in your head.

* Make sure you always do the ritual with an open mind and heart, bringing in genuinely what is to your higher good and not trying to bring in a particular person, which would be an abuse of this power.

* The grid will stay charged for 24 hours. You can recharge it on a daily basis by using the charging crystal and resetting your intention. You can also write your intention on a piece of paper and put it underneath the grid.

Summary

What you focus on is what you create in your life. A ritual is a new habit that changes your focus. A ritual may seem to be an everyday or ordinary act, but it is infused with the spiritual energy of the extraordinary. Regular rituals help you to build belief and expectation that your new life will come about because it changes your focus on every level. Absolute focus from your whole self, conscious and unconscious, cannot fail to bring about change in your life.

There are many kinds of ritual you can introduce into your life as a way of focusing on love attraction.

Your home is itself a symbol of the self, so anything you do to the home will affect you. By carrying out rituals in your home you intentionally make your home into a living ritual since it is the place that carries the vibration of your thoughts every day.

Give each ritual you do proper attention, time and energy. Begin by being clear each time you carry out a ritual what your intention is for that ritual. The spiritual universe will hear that intention and support you in manifesting it. Carrying out the ritual is the action which lets the universe know that you are putting effort into your part of the co-creation process.

Let your rituals be mirrors to the self by making them activities or objects of beauty. You will be rewarded with the flow of love energy into your life.

6: Your Spiritual Helpers

'If you want to be loved, be lovable.'

Ovid

Within the invisible spiritual universe, there are many spiritual helpers (spirit energies), who are available to you. They can be called on to help you discover your repeating patterns that block love. They can support you during difficult times and they can bring you people and opportunities to create love in your life.

You may or may not have worked with spiritual helpers before. The idea of calling on angels or higher guides for help has become very popular over recent years. You may come from a particular religious tradition where you regularly ask a god or goddess for help. If so, you will be familiar with some of the ideas in this chapter. If not, you may be encountering this technique for the first time. You don't have to have done anything before, or belong to any particular faith or religious practice, to turn to these spiritual helpers. They are always there for you.

In this chapter you will learn:

* About three goddesses who will help you with love issues
* How to use goddess power to heal and open your heart
* How to identify your power animal guide
* How to call on angels for help

Calling upon the power of the goddesses

Goddesses are spiritual beings who are there to help us. Whether you are a woman or a man, you can use goddess power to open up your feminine aspect, your attractiveness, your inner and outer beauty and radiance and all aspects of love.

The three goddesses that follow share a similar energy, but each represents a different aspect of this energy. By linking into each of them, you can draw upon their help to heal the parts of you that put a barrier around your heart, and to open up your heart to attract love. You will probably feel that one goddess appeals to you more than the others, even though these are all goddesses through whom you can receive love and healing. Just go with your instinct and draw upon the energy of the one you resonate most with. It will be the energy you most need at this time. Your instinct is always right. Trust it.

For each goddess I have outlined a specific way to draw in their energy through meditation.

Generally it is a good idea to practise the meditation at a time you have put aside for this purpose. However, you don't have to limit yourself to this time. After you have become familiar with the energy of the goddess, you can call on her at any time and use her name to calm yourself or to remind yourself to open up your heart immediately. For example, when you are meeting a new person for the first time, simply ask the goddess to be with you. Or perhaps you are out and about and need help to lift your mood, so again call on her by name.

1: The Goddess Aphrodite

Aphrodite (or Venus in Latin) is the Goddess of Love and Beauty. She is also the goddess of passion and very much associated with sexuality. You can link into her specifically to heal your heart energy and bring new love or passion into your relationships. Her son is Eros (Cupid), who fires the arrows of love and desire into all of us when we meet our romantic partner.

In Greek mythology Aphrodite (Venus) is the daughter of Zeus (Jupiter). The blacksmith god Hephaestus (Vulcan) made her a magic jewelled girdle, which made

> Draw upon a goddess to heal the parts of you that put a barrier around your heart.

her irresistible when she wore it. In Ancient Greece the priestesses of Aphrodite represented her energy, and it was believed that those who slept with them were worshipping the energy of the goddess. Aphrodite herself was said to have had passionate affairs with many mortals and gods, including Adonis and Ares (Mars).

She has several symbols linked to her energy: the swan, dove, scallop shell, flaming torch, mirror, rose, myrtle and also the pomegranate fruit. By linking into her energy, either directly or through focusing on one of her symbols through meditation, you can ask for her help.

How to link to Aphrodite (Venus)

First of all, choose the name you wish to call her – either the Greek Aphrodite or the Latin Venus. They both have slightly different energies, even though the attributes of the goddess in both cultures are basically the same.

Find some space for yourself. Sit quietly and think about how you want to open up your heart to love and passion. Imagine what it will be like when your life is renewed and refreshed and filled with this new feeling. You might also want to ask for help about a very specific old love pattern you used to have in your life and that you now want to fix. Imagine what it will be like when it has gone forever. What will replace it? What will your life be like?

Get into the mood of the love you want to create. Create yourself a loving and romantic atmosphere. You could light candles or even get dressed in clothes that make you

> # Imagine what it will be like when your life is renewed and refreshed.

feel romantic or seductive. Play some romantic music in the background. Think about your favourite romantic novel or film – anything that helps to bring the vibration of Aphrodite's (Venus's) love and passion into the moment.

Then imagine she is in front of you and ask for her help to bring this vibration into your life on a daily basis: 'Dear Goddess Venus, I ask that you now open up my heart to receive all the love, beauty and passion that you can bring. I ask that you now release any blocks, illusions and old patterns of love that hold me back from receiving this beautiful love daily so that I radiate love and attract love, filling my whole being so that I resonate with love and light. I ask that you place your rose within my heart as a symbol of this.'

Now see in your mind's eye a rose in your heart chakra (see page 43) with its petals open to symbolize your open heart. Every morning when you wake up you can remind yourself to open your heart to receive love by visualizing yourself opening up the petals of the rose within your heart.

2: The Goddess Guan Yin

Guan Yin (pronounced gwan-yin in Chinese, sometimes spelt Kwan Yin or in Japanese Kannon) is the Goddess of Love and Compassion. One of the most popular goddesses in Chinese and East Asian traditions, she is the Eastern equivalent of Aphrodite (Venus) and her name means 'she who hears the cries of the world'.

There are many paintings of Guan Yin and you will find her image all over Asia. She is generally shown rather like a Madonna figure, as a

> Guan Yin is a healer, and it is believed that repeating her name will bring her to you in times of need.

beautiful woman in flowing white robes. In her left hand she holds a white lotus, which signifies purity. There are 32 different forms of

Guan Yin. She is often shown as a thousand arms and sometimes a thousand eyes as well, looking in all directions so that she can see and offer mercy to all humanity wherever it is needed.

It is said that Guan Yin was born from a ray of white light that came from the eye of Buddha. Sometimes she carries a vase, which symbolizes compassion and wisdom, a willow branch which symbolizes divine life, or a scroll containing the words of wisdom of Buddha.

How to link to Guan Yin

Ask Guan Yin to help change your love situation by praying to her image or by using a mantra dedicated to her. 'Mantra' means 'to release the mind'. It calls upon the spiritual energies in the universe to change reality on this earth plane (see page 102). Guan Yin is a healer and it is believed by some that even just saying her name again and again will bring her to you in times of need.

If you want to bring Guan Yin's energy into your home, you could create an altar dedicated to her with a statue or picture of her on it or add these to an existing altar. Guan Yin loves water, so place a cup of fresh water there daily. Add flowers as a symbol of the feminine energy she represents.

Chanting Mantras

Mantras are chanted as a way of linking into the energy stirred up by the sound of the words. To begin a chant, sit down, straight-backed on a chair or cross-legged. Exhale stale breath from your body at least three times before you begin the chant, to put yourself into the right state and to relax your mind so that you are ready to receive the new energy into your mind, body, and spirit. Then begin the chant.

When you chant a mantra regularly you do several things. First of all, on a basic level, chanting is a

> ## Chanting links you to pure spiritual consciousness through the energy of words.

form of trance or active meditation. It has the benefits of any kind of meditation, which is to make you feel calmer and more at ease. On a spiritual level, chanting links you to pure spiritual consciousness through the energy of the words expressed in the mantra.

By linking into this energy, you raise your spiritual vibration and expel negative thoughts, opening yourself up to attract blessings and purification.

As you repeat the words again and again, the sound and vibration of the mantra enter your consciousness and the energy of your being. As you say the mantra, other thoughts have no room in your mind, so only the thought of the mantra is present.

The more you repeat the mantra, the more it is felt in rhythmic waves in the body and on a soul level. At a certain point of repetition, you will feel the change taking place as you reach a point of stillness, even of bliss. After you finish chanting, the effect lasts in your body, just as doing a gym session would have lasting effects on your muscle tone even after you leave the gym.

Om mani padme hum

Om mani padme hum (pronounced ohm-mah-nee-pahd-may-hum), or 'Hail to the jewel of the lotus', is my favourite mantra for calling Guan Yin. It is said that if you chant this mantra a million times you will be transformed as you link permanently to the point of pure consciousness within the universe. Luckily, even chanting the mantra consistently will bring changes into your life.

You can begin chanting softly or loudly, inside your head or saying it out loud, again and again. It may not be possible for you to chant out loud in every instance, but it is better if you can do so at least some of the time. This is because the actual sound of the words causes

As you repeat the words the sound and vibration enter your consciousness.

your throat chakra, the energy centre for communication (see page 43), to feel the vibration of the mantra, and the mantra heals and opens up this centre as you chant. The throat chakra may need opening if you have held back from speaking the truth in past relationships or have in any other way suppressed yourself from speaking up for who you are, which is very common in anybody who has attracted unloving situations in the past.

In Tibet *Om mani padme hum* is often inscribed into stones, which are put into buildings as blessings. You can inscribe the mantra on to a personal stone and either carry it with you or put it on a personal altar.

Namo guan shi yin pusa

Namo guan shi yin pusa (pronounced nah-moh-gwan-shir-yin-poo-sah) means 'I call upon the goddess Guan Yin, who observes the cries of the world.'

This is a second mantra you can use to invoke Guan Yin. In this mantra you call on the goddess directly to request help from her. You can ask for help in times of crisis or again simply to set you on the right path to attract more love into your life. Chant the mantra a few times and then ask for the help you need.

3: The Goddess Green Tara

Green Tara is the Tibetan Buddhist equivalent of the Chinese Guan Yin and was originally an Indian goddess. In Japan she is called Tarani Bosatsu (Bosatsu means Buddha). Tara is the female equivalent of the bodhisattva (an enlightened being) called Avalokitesvara. There are many aspects to Tara, of which Green Tara is one of the most loving. The word 'Tara' means 'star' in Sanskrit, and as your star she can provide you with guidance and navigation as you learn to receive love again. Tara is also known as the liberator or saviour.

She symbolizes grace, beauty and also care and protection. She is a goddess who will be there for you in an emergency as she is also a warrior who helps you to fight fear and overcome obstacles. I would encourage you to link with her energy specifically if you feel that you are facing either internal or external obstacles along your path towards attracting love into your life.

Green Tara is a goddess who can really help you to be focused in getting your goals.

She is dressed in silk and jewels and sits on a lotus flower, holding three more in her hand to symbolize the different levels of enlightenment.

> # Green Tara is a goddess who can really help you to be focused in getting your goals.

Om tare tuttare ture soha

Om tare tuttare ture soha (pronounced om-ta-ray-too-ta-ray-too-ray-so-ha) is Tara's mantra. The mantra asks that the goddess liberates you from suffering and helps you to be balanced in your spirituality.

As you chant, imagine your crown chakra on top of your head opening up to let in the white light of the infinite love within the universe and the abundant love of Green Tara, so that it can flow directly into your heart chakra. Make a decision that this love will fill you up so abundantly that you will always have enough to spare for anybody

or anything on the planet that needs love in that particular moment.

This is such a powerful chant that you will feel it reverberate throughout your whole energetic system. Take space each day to meditate on Green Tara if she is the one of the three goddess energies with which you are most in tune.

Remember, when you meditate, wherever possible put yourself in a place free of any distractions, like noise or people walking in on you. The Buddhists call distractions 'meditation thorns', the little day-to-day irritations that take our attention away from the meditation and back to the external world again. Meditation of any form (including chanting) is inner-world work, so keep your space free of mental and physical clutter so that you can turn your attention only to focus on the present moment of connection with the goddess.

> # This powerful chant will reverberate throughout your whole energetic system.

Your power animal guide

Working with animal guides is another wonderful, gentle way to open up your heart energy. You have probably heard of shamans who have animal spirits or of witches who use animal familiars to create magic. Many magical and spiritual traditions have used nature spirits for thousands of years as a way to link into particular vibrations. It is almost like taking a shortcut to a particular destination.

Each of us has some animals that we relate to more than others. You may know of people who collect pictures or images of different animals. For some reason I have

> Spending time in your mind with your heart power animal is a way of opening up to love.

always been drawn to elephants and the great cats. For years I didn't understand why, until I was taken through a 'totem' meditation to discover the animals whose energies most resonated with my heart and spiritual chakras (see page 43) — lo and behold, these very animals! After doing this I was able to work energetically with these animals for spiritual purposes.

Discovering the animal that resonates with your heart is a lovely way to gently feel loving energy open up in your life and it is a very simple thing to discover.

Once you have identified your heart power animal you can bring it out at any time by intentionally relaxing and following this guided meditation. Spending time in your mind with your heart power animal is a way of opening up to love. Keep pictures or even toys in the form of the animal around your home. You can ask it questions; you can ask it to help you to clear spaces of low energy. It will increasingly help you, the more and more you become connected to it. You can call on the energy of your animal guide to be with you any time you need support or are feeling low.

Meet your power animal guide

* Simply sit or lie quietly. Close your eyes and make sure you are comfortable. In your mind's eye open up each of your chakras (see page 43) from the bottom up. See the petals of each chakra opening up to show the beauty of the flower and receive the energy of the universe.

* Now take three deep breaths in through your nose and out through your mouth. As you exhale, feel the breath relax every muscle of your body.

* Feel your legs and arms relax, your fingers and toes and your neck and head relax.

* Imagine that you are walking through a beautiful green meadow into a wood where you can feel the light breeze and smell the scent of the flowers and leaves around you. There are beautiful old and wise trees around you. You are totally connected with nature. You are no different from the flowers or the trees, the sun or the wind.

* Stand still amongst the greenery and imagine you can draw up the energy of the earth through your feet into your body. It is a wonderful loving Mother Earth energy. The energy is drawn up through your feet and then up through each of your chakras. Feel the energy coming up through your lower body, filling it up with love. Draw the energy up to the heart.

* When you reach the heart you will become aware of your heart chakra, located right in the centre of your chest, opening up. As it opens you become aware of an animal there. You may or may not see it immediately or you may become aware of its name before you see it and feel it. Just let it emerge very gently.

* As it emerges, I want you to feel the loving energy of your heart power animal. Talk to it. Be with it. Play with it, touch it, stroke it. Love it.

* Spend time with your animal and then let it return inside you.

* Then let the loving energy in your body expand to fill up every cell of your body. Fill yourself with love and then, when you have done this, simply open your eyes and come back to the room. This is very grounded energy so you should feel peaceful and content.

Help from the angels

An angel is a non-physical being. The name angel means 'messenger of God'. There are many angels who are available to help you and many other guides in the spiritual universe. Like god and goddess spirit energies, angels are available to help you with any area of your life. They also have specializations. The angels who can most help you with love issues are archangels (the highest of the angels) and guardian angels (the angels assigned especially to each of us before we are born). An archangel is a higher form of angel than the guardian angel and so can be called upon when you are in need of extra help.

Archangel Jophiel

All the archangels can help you in many different ways. Archangel Jophiel can help you get out of negative thought patterns, so is a very useful energy when you want to attract love into your life.

Just ask Jophiel for help to make your thoughts more loving, both to yourself and to life in general. Her energy will help this to happen. You can also ask her for help as you start to put your physical home in order. By making your living space more beautiful you are letting her know that you are preparing to welcome in new beauty and love into your

life. Call on her help to make your home a magnet for positive and beautiful thought energies every day.

Your guardian angel

Your guardian angel will stay with you your whole life, but other angels are there only if you call, or 'invoke', them and when you focus on forming a link with them. You don't need to give your guardian angel a name. It is fine just to think of your guardian angel as that.

You can ask your guardian angel to make their presence known to you. You may see the angel in a form that is pleasant to you. You may feel the brush of an angel's wings on your shoulder or back to signal that they are there or feel a tingling on your arm as they connect with you. Your guardian angel may also make their presence known in dreams — look out for helpers appearing in the stories of your dreams.

You can consciously connect with your guardian angel any time just by asking for help. For example, you might say: 'Please help me to achieve this goal' or 'Please help me get the courage I need to sign up to a dating site.'

You can also ask your guardian angel for a sign so that you know that help is coming from the right source. Just say something like:

'Please give me a sign that I am on the right track.'

You may suddenly notice something you haven't noticed before, like an advert that says, 'Sign up now!', or you may just get a strong feeling. The more you practise the connection, the better you will become at noticing these subtle angelic messages.

If you are not sure whether messages are coming from your angels, consider whether they serve your ego or the highest good, not only of you, but of other people around you and the world at large. Messages from the angels will always lead to the latter.

Summary

The spiritual universe is there to help you in your life. There is always help when you need it. Some of the helpers within the spiritual universe to whom you can turn have specific areas of expertise, including the ability to help with relationships or other love issues.

When you want to connect with a particular spiritual being, the more you find out about them, the more you can tune into their energies.

It is very important that you feel drawn to whichever spiritual helper you work with. Find out as much as possible about the three love goddesses in this chapter. Read about them and do your own research. Decide whose energy you most resonate with by paying attention to how you feel when you think about them. When you have decided which one you want to connect to and ask for help around a particular issue, carry out the devotions to them. You can use the suggestions in this chapter or use your instinct to create your own devotions. In return for your devotion, they will help you.

You can forge a separate relationship with your power animal. This is your personal spiritual animal guide. Its energy will stay by you and be a source of comfort and support.

Ask the angels for help every day to make you stronger, to open your heart and to help you through difficult times.

7: Soul Mates

'The minute I heard my first love story,
I started looking for you, not knowing
how blind that was. Lovers don't finally
meet somewhere. They're in each
other all along.'

Rumi

People talk a lot about soul mates. They seem to think that
there's only one special person for all of us and, when they
find this soul mate or 'the one', that will be the end of all
difficulties in life.

If they meet a special person and start having difficulties a
few months into the relationship, then they become really
disillusioned, wondering how this can be the 'right person'
for them if there are issues to be resolved.

When you ask the universe to send you a soul mate, the universe
will oblige, as it will with all your intentions. However, you may
get more than you bargain for. So read on to learn about soul
mates, so that you can make the choice as to whether or not this
is what you really want.

In this chapter you will learn about:
* Soul mates and Karmic ties
* Twin souls
* Dream journeying

The definition of 'soul mate'

I want to start by clarifying terms and being as precise as possible.

Many people use the term 'soul mate' simply to mean a person who will truly love you and whom you will truly love. From the many experiences I have observed I do believe that anyone can at any time consciously attract a deeply connected, loving relationship to them. If this is what you want to create, then I would leave out the words 'soul mate' when you ask the universe to bring you love and ask instead that the universe brings exactly the right person into your life with whom you can be happy, who will be happy with you and with whom you can give and receive love.

You frame this 'cosmic order' or 'intention' by asking that it happens in exactly the right way for you, so that it is part of a balanced happy life in every other way as well and is 'in accord with the highest good to all concerned'.

A true or Karmic soul mate, however, is not the same thing. If you ask for a true soul mate, you will definitely learn through the experience.

Karmic soul mates

A true soul mate is a very special person. He or she is someone with whom you have a deep spiritual bond. This is a bond which has karma attached to it. This means that when you meet them you will experience a deep sense of connection and bonding, but you won't necessarily stay with them for the rest of your life. You may also experience lots of emotions with them that aren't love.

I believe that many true soul mates have the potential to come into our lives, although it is also possible that you will meet only one in a lifetime. When you meet your Karmic soul mate you both come into each other's lives to teach each other something. You are both here to teach and both here to learn. Through this meeting you are given the opportunity by the universe to understand yourself and your purpose on a deeper level and to grow both spiritually and emotionally.

Meeting a Karmic soul mate and walking your life with them for a short or long time can be the most amazing healing experience you will ever have. They may shift you further along in your life than ever before. Through a true soul mate you can learn to love for the first time, love more deeply or learn any soul lesson that you need. However, I do believe that it is not necessary that a true soul mate is your mate for life. He or she can be. I have seen people meet, part and then come back together after years and stay together forever in total happiness. I have also seen a true soul mate manifested for a short time in a life and then leave after whatever lesson needs to be learned has been learned.

Karmic ties

Karmic soul mates come from the same group of souls within the spiritual universe. We reincarnate with them across many lifetimes. Karmic ties are formed between souls in these previous lives. They happen when deep emotions have attached two people together. A Karmic soul mate may have been your lover, but also your brother, your mother or your father.

You may have loved each other. One of you may have loved the other and the other have hated. A Karmic soul mate may have been your enemy as much as your closest friend in a previous lifetime. It is said that any deep emotional bond will link you together across time and space. When the person reappears in this lifetime the karma or lesson from the previous lifetime needs to be resolved. You make this contract with your Karmic soul mate before you are born into this life.

If there has been a Karmic love bond across different lifetimes,

when you meet this person they will appear like a whirlwind in your life. Their appearance may disrupt your life and appear to cause problems at first, but if it is a true soul-mate

> Be ready to hear and observe what you need to know about love.

relationship then there is nothing you can do. For example, if you are already in a relationship and a Karmic soul mate appears, then undoubtedly the relationship will be affected. What exactly will happen depends on what the Karmic soul mate has come into your life to teach you on a spiritual level. Your existing relationship may or may not survive. The more important issue will be that you do not resist the lessons, but are ready to hear and observe what you need to know about love – for ultimately the lesson a Karmic soul mate brings is always one about love and healing.

What is important about Karmic soul mates is that you learn and grow and evolve together. Not all the lessons will be comfortable. This is because many of us resist unconditional love in favour of hanging on to what we know. What we resist persists. Love always finds a way through eventually and that is the lesson. Along the way, you will learn forgiveness of self and others, probably slowly, until experience eventually helps you to recognize what you need to understand much more quickly. This is because we always have free will and choice to play the victim for a while, or behave in an unloving way to others.

How will you know whether you are learning from the lesson a Karmic soul mate is bringing? The only measure is love. If you are in pain, you are in lack and not in love. However, if you can move from pain or suffering through forgiveness to love, then you can live a lifetime with a Karmic soul mate in true joy.

Twin souls

The term 'twin souls', or 'twin rays', is another description that you may come across. Many people believe that a twin soul is the other half of your soul, which has been divided into two. The soul experiences life on the earth as male and female (yang and yin), so your twin soul appears in the opposite gender to you.

When you meet your twin soul, this is what many people mean as the 'one'. You have the feeling of being totally whole for the first time in your life. There will be a strong psychic bond between the two of you. You may really feel that you

understand what the other person feels or is about to say. You will feel a deep love and trust. Again, there are as many theories about twin souls as there are about soul mates.

It is possible that we do not get the chance to meet a twin soul until we have learned the lessons of many true soul-mate encounters because we won't be ready. A twin soul can only come into your life if you have grown sufficiently on a spiritual level to be ready for this intense relationship. A twin-soul relationship is based only on love, so won't come if you generally operate out of neediness, ego, or anger.

Divine purpose

It is said that when you meet your twin soul, it is not just to experience love on this earth, but to fulfil a divine purpose. When twin souls come together their experience on this earth is magnified. They are able to achieve more than each could separately, not necessarily in terms of material success, but with a purpose that brings more love to the world.

When you meet your twin soul, you will be filled with unconditional love. Sometimes people become obsessed with another person. They need to be with them 24 hours a day and to know what they are doing and feeling and thinking. They assume this is because this is the 'one' who is meant for them. However, this is not a twin-soul situation. Life with a twin soul is never co-dependent. You aren't needy of each other. It is certainly intense because you have met the 'other half' of you. However, it is always unconditional, and you find that you are able to be utterly honest with each other because you don't wish to judge each other in any way. Indeed, any neediness you may have experienced in past relationships will be replaced by a common desire to grow together emotionally and spiritually. Your souls know that you have a bond that will outlast life on this earth.

Not all of us will meet a twin soul in our lifetimes, nor would we wish to as we are not all spiritually ready. Most of us will meet Karmic soul mates and go through many experiences and lessons. As we do this we grow and experience more and more love in our lives each time. We become stronger in our sense of self, and happier. There are always ups and downs in life, but the more we learn how to let go of problems and receive love, the more our lives will be filled with love. Don't worry about making mistakes in your relationships or picking the wrong person. As long as you become open to unconditional love it will find you because it is within you.

Dream journeying

If you yearn for a true soul mate or twin-soul experience, you can bring it into your life through dream journeying.

Your soul is free to travel at night and meet other souls. Once you establish contact with another soul in your dream world, you can ask him or her to come to you in the physical world. You have only to desire it to happen and it will. Remember, though, there is always a time lag.

We are often given more than one opportunity to meet our true soul mate. If we don't take it and it is an important connection, then luckily the same person will come back.

I would also say that it is important always to be open when somebody comes into your life. Significant love connections don't announce themselves with a big flag on them saying: 'Hey, I am your soul mate' or 'Hey, I am your twin soul.' First appearances can be very deceptive. A bond that is so clear on the dream plane has to get past all your unconscious prejudices and defences on the earth plane. Your true soul mate may be very slim while you have always been physically attracted to people who are a little cuddlier. If that's the case, then make sure you look past the superficial or you might miss out on someone who can love you forever (perhaps in more than one lifetime).

If you do keep an open mind then eventually the love bond on the dream plane will draw you together and you will recognize each other. Clearly, though, it is much easier if you don't put up lots of barriers to begin with.

Like attracts like

By the way, you have no doubt heard people say 'opposites attract'. Well, a soul mate doesn't work like that. It works on a 'like attracts like basis.' When you meet a Karmic soul mate or your twin soul, then it is going to be because you are alike on a deep soul level. You may speak different languages, live in different countries, come from different cultural and wealth backgrounds or have very different jobs, but on a soul level there will be a basic likeness that binds you together. The more you get to know each other through love, the more you will discover that mirror within each of you.

Your dream journey to meet your karmic soul mate

Remember, when you desire something, focus on it with all your attention and it will come to you. This is the Law of Attraction. Ask each night before you go to sleep that you meet the right person to be with you in this lifetime and at this point in your life. Ask that you see him or her and talk to him or her. I use this language very precisely so that whoever manifests brings you the life experiences you need at this time.

If you can lucid dream, as I hope you will find easy with practice, then tell your Karmic soul mate where you live and ask that he/she comes to you. Then hand the manner in which this happens over to the spiritual universe, trusting that it knows much better than us what soul experiences we need at this time on earth. You can, however, ask that this be speeded up 'under divine law' and that the universe removes any obstacles to that happening immediately.

You can also ask that your true soul mate gives you some message or means of identifying himself or herself on the earth plane (although this doesn't always happen, as part of your lesson may be to learn to recognize your true soul mate).

Get used to doing this regularly so that when you meet this true soul mate you are very familiar with their energies. This will make you much more able to identify them when you do meet on the earth plane.

Personally, I like to add one more request, although this comes with a health warning as well. I ask that any lessons I need to learn that are preventing me from meeting my true soul mate at once are given to me immediately — in other words, 'bring it on'. These lessons are going to bring me experiences that aren't always comfortable (that's why they are lessons), but are necessary for my spiritual growth, so personally I would rather get them all out of the way in this lifetime. You can choose to do the same or not. It depends how much spiritual growth you are up for this time around! (I always was a bit of a swot at school and now I have become an ambitious spiritual one, too!)

Recognizing your Karmic soul mate/twin soul

Recognition is not necessarily instant. The only way to recognize your mate is to feel, not think. At a certain point in your relationship you will have a feeling that begins with familiarity and trust and then opens up to love. This familiarity comes from the fact that you have met before, on the dream plane and in other lifetimes.

If you are forced apart for any reason, then you feel the loss very clearly in your heart chakra (see page 43). (This is very different from the loss of someone you are obsessed with or needy of, but don't actually love — when the loss is felt in the solar plexus chakra.)

The heaven-sent marriage

When you finally meet on the earth plane your Karmic soul mate/twin soul you have met in your dreams, you have the opportunity because of the deep bond to overcome past Karmic lessons and bring about a blissful union, which is sometimes referred to as the 'heaven-sent marriage'.

This will not happen straight away. There are two ways we can come together with another person: on a soul level or a personality level. The desires of the personality can get in

> Recognition is not necessarily going to be instant.

the way of love and a soul bond. The personality may want that tall, dark handsome man. The soul wants the short, blond man. If the personality digs its heels in, then the soul has to wait until the personality issues are resolved.

Your heaven-sent marriage is going to take work and commitment. That's why not all true soul-mate unions are forever. If you still have thoughts and beliefs that reject love, you are going to need to keep healing them, otherwise your true soul mate will mirror them back to you.

If you feel anger, then that's your personality playing up. Take note of what's going on and the thoughts that are coming up. Are they lack thoughts or abundant thoughts (see page 14)?

If you feel depressed, then you are putting out too much energy and thinking about what other people think of you. If you feel rejected, then you are rejecting yourself. These are all personality issues and do not come from the soul. It is your wrong thinking and illusions that bring pain, not your true soul mate.

When you feel that there is someone for you in times of emotional or spiritual hardship, then that is caused by the souls of you and your mate touching each other and supporting each other. Life with a true soul mate won't always be bliss, but it will always be held together by this deep feeling of love.

When you meet your right mate and see beyond the day-to-day trivial disputes brought about by the personality, it's as if you both now have a foundation under your lives. You can never fall through that foundation. Whatever happens, your love operates as a support there to catch you. You come together, grow together, find passion together and purpose together.

Summary

The future you want comes about partly through your own creation and partly through the creation of the universe. At times the universe gives you opportunities to learn as a way of developing as a spiritual being. One of these ways is to bring people into your life who can teach you something you haven't had the opportunity to learn before or have not been willing to learn. We talk about soul mates, but this is a much misused and misunderstood word. Do you really want a true karmic soul mate in your life? Have you met a twin soul? Have you met someone you think might be a karmic soul mate?

If you think that you have or want this experience, be open and willing to learn from what happens. Recognize that your experience isn't necessarily going to be easy, but it will be to your higher good. Ask the universe what this person brings to you in terms of learning for your spiritual development. Remember they may or may not stay in your life, but the knowledge you gain from the experience will stay with you whatever happens.

8: Get Ready For Love

'There are two ways to live your life.
One is as though nothing is a miracle.
The other is as though everything is a
miracle.'

Albert Einstein

Okay, so what now? You may have already found that things
have changed. Or maybe the change hasn't quite happened yet.
Or perhaps a lot of change has happened. What do you do next?

Change is a journey. It may happen in small incremental steps,
or it may happen all in one day when you least expect it. I don't
know which way it will happen for you because we are all
different. All I can tell you is that, if you make a change within
yourself, it is impossible that there will not be some change as
a consequence in your life.

Internal change equals external change. As soon as you take
action towards a new future, the new future is on its way.

In this chapter you will learn about:

* Trusting the universe
* The love-attraction checklist
* Happy endings

When will my new future happen?

'When?' is the question I am most frequently asked. How long do I need to wait? This depends partly on your belief system and any timing you have set for your vision to manifest, and partly on the rules we all operate under as human beings. You are of course a human being and a human being, in the world of matter, operates according to the rules of time and space.

Of course, if you really think about it, thank goodness that we do have

> As soon as I was really clear about what I wanted, and why, the universe responded.

time and space in this universe. If I ask for a new home, kitchen, lover, job, or whatever, do I really want them all tumbling down my chimney in one go? Would I be ready to have my future all in one go? From my experience, change happens at exactly the time I am ready for it, even though I often long to speed things up.

Nevertheless, I am certain I am not alone in having found this enormously frustrating at times. Everyone I know who consciously

does any kind of manifestation technique gets frustrated waiting. But sometimes time and space help us. Things happen at particular times because the universe really does appear to know when the time is right. We may really want something to happen immediately, but that doesn't mean that it is necessarily the best thing for us. Actually, the universe has tested me several times over the years. I have met someone twice in the past and not noticed them, then years later met them when I was ready to be with them. I was offered wealth at a time it meant nothing to me and rejected it, then when I wanted it again, I appreciated it much more for the time I had spent without it. Why did it happen when it did? Well, my beliefs really needed to change and as soon as I had put the effort into changing them and getting really clear about what I wanted, and why that was really right for me, the universe responded immediately.

I know, I know. You're still thinking, 'But I am ready now!'

All I can say is please really trust. Trust that a transformation in your life is under way now. Trust that the universe knows the right timing for you. You are already stepping into a new reality — a reality you have asked for. Be patient. Trying to push things to happen or being over-attached to your outcome won't bring it nearer faster. A gentle focus on what you want to bring into your life is quite enough.

Be patient

Now, align yourself to your future with gratitude to allow the flow of love and abundance into your life. Believe that it has already fully manifested in your life.

Trust is enough. Once you have planted the seeds of your thoughts in the universe, the universe knows what you want and is already changing the circumstances of your life. It's just like when you plant a seed in your garden, there are all sorts of things you can't see happening under the ground, but when the earth is ready to receive the flower, up it comes.

> Once you have planted the seeds of your thoughts, the universe knows what you want.

Carry on with your life, finding new enthusiasms and new times for fun and joy. Carry on noticing all the blessings you already have in your life. Step by step, piece by piece, you are creating the life you have always wanted, bringing towards you more and more of the experiences you always dreamed of having and changing into the person you always intended to be. Be patient and allow the universe to open up your miraculous new beginning for you.

When in doubt...

But what if you doubt? What if it is taking too long? What if you think it will happen, but you don't absolutely know that it will happen? Or you think that you may know, but you aren't certain if you know you know ... and so on?

Yes, it's hard to read and make sense of those sentences. It is even more muddling when they are thoughts going round and round in your brain. If you start doubting or being not sure, or getting confused, or over-analyzing or getting in any other way stuck about what you think you can manifest in your life, I want you to just stop. Take a big deep breath and go back to basics.

Opposite is a final checklist to enable you to make sure that you attract the most wonderful life.

The love-attraction checklist

* Check where, and if, you are really stuck. Reread the chapters that can be most helpful to you. Check out the Love-attraction Formula (see page 8). Notice if there is anything you have forgotten to do or whether there are any steps you have missed or rushed through.

* Check your beliefs. Do you believe it is OK to attract love? Do you believe that you deserve to attract love? Do you believe you can attract love? Have you let go of lack and woken up to a new way of thinking that you can attract an abundance of love into your life as much as anyone else?

* Check that you have healed what you needed to have healed. Have you truly forgiven who and what needs to be forgiven in your life, including yourself? Have you noticed the good things you have learned from the past as well as the things you no longer wish to keep?

* Check your intention. Do you have a clear vision of what you are going to bring into your life? Do you have pictures – either on your love treasure map (see page 49–50) or in your mind's eye, or both – of the sort of life you will be living when it is filled with love? Are you certain that you believe this is possible and probable, so that it has moved from a 'want' to a 'when'?

＊

＊ Check your own self-love. What do you really feel about yourself? Be totally truthful. I don't just mean when you are feeling at your best, but every day, no matter who is present or not present in your life.

＊ Check your daily habits. Have you built into your life regular rituals that help you to maintain the belief that you are going to attract this love into your life? Have you identified your power animal of the heart? Have you decided which form of the love goddess you are most in tune with? If so, have you asked for help? Make it a habit. Build your connection with the spiritual universe and the energies will come closer to you and help you every day in your life.

＊ Check your dreams. What is going on in them? Are they indicating how near you are to attracting your new life? Are they indicating any blocks to be resolved or any thought patterns still present that need a bit of change? If so, make the change. Have you tried waking dreaming? If 'no', give it a go. If 'yes', how regularly? Take a week and use waking dreaming to build your dreams. Flow your feelings into them and let them become a magnet for love.

Happy endings

Finally, I want to take you back to Lucy, whom I told you about on page 25. Change happened to Lucy when she first started using the Law of Attraction. She rang me up out of the blue about a year after she had started making changes in her thinking.

A year previously, we had sat in a café and Lucy had described the life she wanted with a wonderful man who would love her for who she was. We talked through what she wanted for over an hour, but I could

> Build your connection with the spiritual universe and the energies will come closer to you.

tell she wasn't totally certain that she could really create this change in her life. However, something was set in motion because a few months later she started to make changes one after another.

First, Lucy made the decision to move to a different house as she had stayed in the house where she had lived with her husband. She had thrown out all her old clutter, then she started buying new clothes and new furniture. There were very few

men in her life at this time. She was surrounded by single women who were constantly complaining about the terrible time they had gone through with men. As soon as she moved house, which was a huge decision for her, she got offered the chance of a new career as well. She started going out and meeting lots of new people and getting her confidence back. She didn't meet a boyfriend immediately, but was already much happier.

Then one day Lucy gave me a call. 'The strangest thing has happened,' she said. 'I had just stopped looking for a man and I had decided to get on with my life. Actually I just thought life is too short to worry any more and I decided to be happy with what I had. It was almost a year to the day when I made that decision that I got an email. I was going to delete it because I didn't recognize the address and thought it might be spam. Something made me open it.'

The email was from a former boyfriend of Lucy's from many years ago – Bob, the last boyfriend she had had before she had met and married Steven. They had been together for a year or so, but then Bob had moved abroad to do voluntary work and, this being before everybody had email and used Facebook, they had lost touch. It turned out that Bob had been trying to track down Lucy for a whole year — again, amazingly around the time Lucy had sat in the café with me talking about the kind of life she wanted. He had sent a card to her old family address, he had emailed old friends, but no one was in touch with her.

Bob was about to give up when he managed to track down an old girlfriend of Lucy's. Although she hadn't been in touch with Lucy for a while herself, she did give him Lucy's email.

There is a real fairy-tale happy ending here. Lucy was very nervous about meeting Bob again after so many years, but when she did, it felt so natural to both of them being together that they moved in together after only three months.

'I just knew it was safe to be with him because he loved me before,' Lucy told me, 'but also because I had been through all those big changes by myself over the last year. I felt braver about life and I knew that it was safe to be myself with someone again.'

Summary

Now that you have reached the end of this section my wish for you is that your story has a happy ending as well.

Take all the time you need to change your life and make it how you want to be.

Learn through practice how the Law of Attraction can bring love into your life every day.

Change the story of your past to a happy one. Recognize the perfect, loving being you are. Start now with a fresh sheet of paper and begin to dream the life you want to create.

Look to the spiritual universe and the helpers who live within it to help you realize your dream of a loving future.

Rely on the Law of Attraction as a perfect means of bringing the future you want into your life.

Set your intention to co-create your future and show your commitment to the universe by taking action towards what you want every day.

＊

What if the Law of Attraction doesn't work for you?

＊ Change the timescale. Let go of the date or push your date forward. A watched kettle seldom boils. By over-watching results, you push the outcome you want further away.

＊ Allow enough time for your future to manifest.

＊ Remember that you can't see the workings of the universe any more than you can see a seed beginning to grow under the earth. When you think nothing is happening there may be something going on that you need to pay attention to.

＊ Then, if you still aren't getting what you want, change something. Change what you are thinking, doing or seeking to create.

＊ Look for unconscious, unloving thought patterns focused on lack rather than abundance. If any are still there, change them.

＊ Pay particular attention to the thoughts you have about relationships. Forgive the past, yourself and people who have hurt you.

＊ Notice if you have a clear enough picture of your future.

* Establish whether your picture is good for you and all around you. Make sure it brings balance into your life by questioning why you really want this.

  * Take different actions towards your new future and see what happens.

  * Use ritual to reinforce your intentions for your life.

    * Change your home to reflect the new you.

* Notice the 'mirrors' around you and the people coming into your life. As your life begins to change, one of the first clues is seen in the people you attract.

  * Pay attention to your night-time dreams. If you find it easier, use daytime meditation to seek messages from the spiritual universe.

    * Forge a relationship with a love goddess and let her help you.

* Finally, if you have done everything, then trust. Trust is an abundant thinking pattern. Trust and let go, relying totally on the universe to bring you, if not exactly what you have asked for, definitely a future that is even more to your higher good.

Manifesting

PROSPERITY

1: Find Your Flow

'As a man thinketh in his heart, so he is.'

Proverbs 23:7

This chapter is about giving and receiving. Is it better to do one or another to create prosperity? The universe is essentially a world of balance and harmony. To tap into its abundant flow of energy and prosperity, you need to find a balance between giving and receiving, outward flow and inward flow. At the same time, it is important to let the universe know that you are aware of the blessings you already have in your life, so that it is clear exactly what you would like it to help you to manifest in the future.

In this chapter you will learn:

* How to be grateful for what you already have
* How to tap into the universe's flow of abundance
* About the Law of Balance
* How to receive and when to give

A lesson in receiving

When I was about nine, I was offered the chance to be a star at school. I had a good singing voice, and each year we put on some kind of performance for our parents. I had never made it beyond playing a minor-league rat in the *Pied Piper of Hamelin*, so this was my chance to shine. What's more, I knew that I really wanted to be up there singing and acting and entertaining. This was my big break. My teacher came up to me and in a very kind voice asked me if I would like to take a big singing role in the next production. Of course, I wanted to. I was smaller and younger than a lot of the other people in my class. This would make me important and popular, wouldn't it? So naturally — or so it seemed to me — I said no.

I did not say no because I did not want the part. I said no because somehow, I had got it into my head that it was impolite to say yes straight away to things you wanted. I have no idea where this idea came from. I do not remember anyone ever telling me this, but somehow, I associated saying yes immediately with being greedy or arrogant. What I wanted to happen next was for my nice teacher to ask me again and persuade me that I really did want to participate, so that I could graciously accept with my honour intact. Sadly, that was not what

happened. Instead, my teacher turned to my best friend, and asked her to do it instead. Of course, my best friend, having no such hang-ups, said yes immediately — and I went home in tears.

I would like to tell you that I learned from this experience but, unfortunately that was not the case. It has taken me years and years to wake up to the fact that not everyone expects to ask a second time or to press you into accepting their generosity. In fact, sometimes there will be no generosity at all unless you ask. That is a particularly hard pill for me to swallow because, you see, pride comes in at that point. I grew up in poor circumstances, which meant that a lot of our family's time was spent covering up our need, not telling the world about it. I do not know what your beliefs are about receiving, but I urge you to think about them. You see, the universe will always press

Sometimes there will be no generosity at all unless you ask.

your buttons a bit. It is going to bring you prosperity; however, if you need to learn a lesson about prosperity and the way in which to bring it into your life, then it may be that you receive that lesson in the way in which prosperity is offered to

If you show the universe you are not comfortable with the small gifts it brings, it will not bring you other, more substantial gifts.

you. When I was young, I had to learn how to separate other people's generosity from the idea of 'charity'. I had to swallow my pride and not only learn to accept help, but also to do it graciously and with genuine gratitude.

What are your attitudes toward receiving? You may think that you want the universe to give more to you, but are you always happy to receive in the moment? Do you hold any misguided, conflicting or inappropriate beliefs or attitudes about when and how it is right to receive? It would be nice and simple if the universe just handed each one of us a lottery ticket or financial windfall, but that is unlikely to happen. It is much more likely that you will come by wealth in an everyday fashion: through investments, a salary, friends, family

gifts or inheritance, or selling a business. Would it matter to you if you inherited money? Would you be OK if you received a gift of a lot of money from a friend or romantic partner?

If you show the universe, you are not comfortable with the small gifts it brings – in the form of compliments or opportunities or small gifts of money – it will not give you other, more substantial gifts because you have rejected its generosity. A good place to change any mixed beliefs about receiving is by learning to be grateful for what you already have in your life.

Gratitude every day

How often have you heard the expression 'Count your blessings'? I was brought up in the United Kingdom. I am lucky to have been born in a country that is one of the most affluent in the world and where I have had the freedom to choose the career I want and to move freely to other countries to work as well. I did not have children or a family to constrain me when I was travelling, so I could make the decision to travel to where I thought I would learn the most and earn the most.

Many religious or spiritual rituals, whatever the origin, start by giving thanks to a god or higher being for all that has been provided. 'For what we are about to receive may we be truly grateful' is just one example of this. Many practices also end with words such as 'Thanks be to God' or something similar.

Do you say some form of a blessing before eating? Even if you were not brought up in this way, you can still learn the power of saying thank you. This happened for me when I lived in Japan, where it is traditional to say '*itadakimasu*' (literally, 'I humbly receive') before a meal. No doubt you have encountered or read about similar practices in many households around the world, if not in your own.

Gratitude is an emotion. There have been many studies in psychology on gratitude and its effects. What is clear is that two people who experience exactly the same life circumstances can and will react in very different ways. Imagine that someone in your life has done you a favour. How do you react? The amount of gratitude you feel is not fixed at some standard level. It is determined by the value you put on what you receive, how you perceive the intentions of the person who has given it to you and what you perceive the cost is to the other person.

Our interpretation leads us to value or undervalue what we receive.

Why is it important to be grateful for what you already have?

It is very important to feel grateful for everything you receive from other people and for your life in general. It is important to give thanks to the universe because everything you have in your life right now is a gift.

Saying thank you for the things we receive every day is a very powerful process. It reminds us what an abundant world we live in and how generous the universe is toward us. Every time we say thank you for what we have already received, we acknowledge that the universe is

> Saying thank you for the things we receive every day is a very powerful process.

there to help us. It has our best interests at heart. Whatever we have now is enough for us in this moment, whether or not we know it at this time.

If you want to create more all you have to do is to thank God or the universe, whatever you like to call the divine source of all creation, for what has been provided for you already, then ask in addition for what you would like as well.

Thanking the universe in advance for what you are about to receive shows your faith in the universe that your wishes will be fulfilled. This keeps you in a prosperity mindset, allowing the Law of Attraction (see page 11) to work for you. It prevents you from falling into lack thinking and poverty consciousness (see page 14).

Start your own daily gratitude habit

Adopt a little ritual of counting your blessings and actually saying thank you out loud once a day. Take a little bit of time out of the day — I find the end of the day works best but choose the time that feels most right to you. What is key is that you make this a conscious and consistent daily practice.

As you think through what has happened to you over the course of the preceding day, think of at least three things for which you are really grateful. Do not just pay lip service to the universe. Really consider the blessings the day has brought you, even if it has been a tough day at work or at home. Do not discount some of the things you might usually take for granted. You probably still have a roof over your head. Or a bed to sleep in. Or food on the table.

Recognize the value of what each

second of the day has given you. Even if it has not been an easy day, think about the life lessons you are getting that will really help you later in life.

Now think about how you have helped to bring about each of these blessings and thank God or the universe for supporting you in this by giving you the circumstances and the means by which this has happened. Thank God or the universe for the friends you have around you, your job, the money you earned today, or the space you had to think and dream. There will always be something you can find, no matter your circumstances. In fact, I have met extraordinarily poor people who can always find something for which to give thanks.

> ## Count your blessings and say thank you out loud once a day.

As you begin to identify the blessings in your life, you will give yourself the means to attract more and more until your day is filled with blessings. Actually, it already is filled with blessings. You just may not have quite noticed yet. As you begin to imagine your prosperous future (see Decide Your Prosperous Future, pages 138–156), remember to be grateful in advance for the joyous creation that the universe is bringing to you.

The Law of Balance

This is a harmonious universe. This is echoed in visual symbols of the world from great spiritual traditions such as Daoism and Tantra, in the yin/yang and the Wheel of Life, where you will see that the universe is always in balance. We live in a world of matter that is sometimes called the 'manifest universe' — as opposed to the 'invisible' or 'spirit' universe, which is also called the 'unmanifest universe'. The unmanifest universe is the place of creation. When an idea is seeded as a dot or a spark of creation in the spirit universe, it eventually becomes reality in the manifest universe. It is able to exist in the manifest universe only 'in polarity'. This means that, for it to exist, its opposite must exist as well. For every black there is a white. For every light there is shadow. This way the universe always remains in balance.

The Chinese symbol representing yin and yang shows this beautifully. The two sides of the symbol perfectly balance each other. One is dark and one is light. One is hot and the other cold. In traditional Chinese medicine, both yin and yang 'winds'

exist within the body. If you become either too 'hot' or too 'cold', this will manifest as discomfort or illness.

The Tree of Life found in the Western mystery tradition is another illustration of a similar idea. One side of the tree is female. One side of the tree is male. One is dark and one is light. The Tree of Life is a map of all existence. It shows the structure underlying every aspect of the universe. When a spark of creation is born into the world, it moves from the top of the tree down to the bottom of the tree. The path it takes is known as the 'lightning strike'. It zigzags from one side of the tree to the other, not in a straight line, taking on the energies of both sides and keeping perfectly in balance.

This is quite a complex subject, but what it means, put simply, is that the universe likes balance. If we have balance, we feel good. If we are unbalanced, we have to get back into balance. On a large scale you can see this in the way that economic cycles work. If we all spend too much and go into debt, eventually the cycle corrects itself and we all have to stop spending and start saving to get back into balance. People work in the same way. Sometimes you have up cycles and sometimes you have down cycles. The more you can keep your life in balance, the smoother those cycles will be.

How does this apply to prosperity

In the natural world many processes are in a state of flux. On a universal scale, by its very definition the universe is never static, but rather in a constant cycle of ebb and flow. Prosperity is no different. If you give, you also need to receive to keep in balance. An abundant universe means that you can let go and give freely, knowing that you will always have enough because you will receive back what you have given and more. Even monks or hermits do this. They may have few or no material possessions, but they agree with the universe that they will give and receive spiritual energy as a counterbalance to their needs being fulfilled. This free flow works automatically as long as your beliefs allow you to both receive and give.

> If you wish to receive, you need to give as well.

If your beliefs block this flow, your life will not be in balance. Look what happens to misers who hoard their gold. Do they live happily? They may not lose their money, but perhaps their life will suffer in other ways. The classic Dickens tale *A Christmas Carol* illustrates this beautifully. Scrooge was friendless and lonely as a miser until he learned his lesson and gave generously to Tiny Tim's family, immediately opening the door to love and friendship. If you hold on tightly and hoard because you are afraid there is not enough to go around, you stop the flow of abundance, and your life will not be prosperous in the true sense because of this imbalance. It was the English philosopher and scientist Francis Bacon (1561–1626) who first said, 'Money is like muck [manure], not good except it be spread.'

How to find your flow

It is very simple. If you wish to receive, you need to give as well. Equally, if you give, you need to receive as well. If you do not pay attention to both giving and receiving, you will inevitably get out of balance. All prosperity is granted to us from the universe. We pay for it in one form or another.

You may wonder why a neighbour or friend has money and you do not. After all, he or she does not appear to be giving to charity or taking care of anybody. Maybe not, but wherever wealth is gained there is some energy exchange going on. Work is one form of energy we give in exchange for money. If you focus on creating wealth — and your beliefs allow it — then money will come your way.

Does having money mean that you need to give it all away to maintain balance? No. Money is only another form of energy. What you do need to do is to think about whether you use that money wisely in the world and how you live your life.

Tithing

In the Judeo-Christian tradition, it has long been understood that it is good to give as well as to receive, and this is how the concept of tithing was born. To 'tithe' means to give away ten percent of what you earn. The word comes from the Old English word *teogatha*, which literally means 'one tenth'. A tithe was historically a voluntary contribution, but also sometimes a tax paid to a religious organization. Tithes in England were not necessarily cash payments, but more often payments 'in kind', such as food offerings. In Europe barns were built across the land to house the agricultural tithe. In traditional Jewish religious practice, tithing has gone on for hundreds of years, with followers of the religion giving away ten percent of their income to charity.

Borrowing wealth

Offerings at Chinese temples follow the same principle of giving back. You make a beautiful present of flowers or hard-earned food to the gods, and in return they give you something, be it blessings or good luck. In China and throughout Chinese-influenced Asia, the goddess Guan Yin (see pages 101–103), the goddess of mercy, is given offerings at her temples in return for her blessings.

Legends say that there were once five hundred guardian angels who wanted to test the extent of Guan Yin's abundance. They disguised themselves as monks and went to her temple to ask for food. The bountiful goddess did not hesitate to give them all food. In gratitude, the angels took some of the food and gave the excess to ordinary people who were hungry because there is always excess available to give. Nowadays, the Chinese go to Guan Yin's temple to ask for blessings, including blessings of wealth. The day to do this is on the 26th day of lunar January, a day that is marked in Chinese calendars as the 'Day of Borrowing Wealth from Guan Yin'. It is seen as borrowing because it is recognized that you should give back something in return for what you receive. If you ask for wealth, you must also be prepared to give something in return, although you do not have to do this the same day. Whether or not you get exactly what you ask for, in Chinese practice, at the end of the lunar year you go back to the temple to return your wealth because a promise is a promise, and a contract is a contract. You give something back to the goddess on this day, be it your thanks and prayers or offerings.

Put your money where your mouth is

The idea of giving and receiving as a way of getting into the flow of abundant thinking has already been discussed in the book (see page 134). You can form rituals around giving as a way of cementing your belief in an abundant universe.

Using real money really builds your faith and trust, so I would encourage you to make your own rituals of money sacrifice, knowing that this will help the flow of prosperity. Take a look at Prosperity Rituals (pages 173–187) for suitable rituals you can use.

If you are developing a relationship with a particular god or goddess associated with abundance and prosperity or general luck in life (see Your Prosperity Helpers, pages 188–202), you can donate money to an organization or temple associated with this particular spiritual power. If not, perhaps you can tithe a percentage of your money to an organization that has associations with the ideas you want to bring into your life. For example, if you are going to use your wealth to help nature, donate to an environmental cause. Businesses that are asking clients to pay for a service will often add a voluntary charitable donation. I do not think that this is the best way to go about things energetically, because it should be you making the sacrifice if you are the business, rather than requiring it of your customers. Instead, decide your fee, then donate to the organization of your choice. Physically handling the cash as you give it away will carry a higher energetic association for you than if you make a credit-card payment. The idea is that it should feel as if you are making a sacrifice, so that you feel the connection to your intention to create prosperity.

Enjoy your money

Just having money piled up in a bank or under the mattress does not build prosperity consciousness. Use your money to give yourself pleasure, and you are telling yourself that you deserve to receive good things by creating a flow of wealth. Enjoy spending your money on the things that make you feel good.

At the same time, stop spending

for spending's sake. Some people develop a bit of an addiction to the act of buying. They go out and spend money because the act of buying something makes them feel good, even though they do not really want what they buy. A few minutes later all the pleasure is gone, and they are left with a feeling of guilt, or 'buyer's regret'. Any addiction means that you have an unhealthy relationship with whatever it is that you are addicted to. In the case of spending for spending's sake, you are telling yourself that you will never have enough stuff or that 'enough is never enough'. Give yourself a cooling-off period before buying something, to help you to change your habits. If you can, stop buying anything nonessential for a week or a month, and instead use some of the rituals and exercises found throughout the book to change your relationship with money.

Summary

Take time each day to examine what has happened and count your blessings. Pick at least three things you are grateful for that day. At the same time, express your thanks to the universe for the positive, prosperous future it is bringing to you — even if it has not arrived in your life quite yet.

Learn to give generously, while at the same time being open to receiving. If you find one or the other easier, practise opening yourself up to the flow of the abundant universe.

As you continue reading through the book, use other techniques and rituals to reinforce your positive abundant thinking. Consider tithing or a similar physical expression of generosity, so that you demonstrate to the universe your faith that wealth and prosperity will continue to flow into your life.

2: Decide Your Prosperous Future

'I am no bird; and no net ensnares me:
I am a free human being with an
independent will.'

Charlotte Bronte, *Jane Eyre*

This chapter is all about learning how to create a vision for your future and breaking it down into individual goals. Your decisions will create your prosperous future. In order to create not only money, but also happiness alongside it, it is important to be clear about what you want and why you want it. The 'why' will alert you to what is lacking in your life, while the 'what' clarifies where you will put your focus.

In this chapter you will learn:

* Why money is not the same as prosperity
* How to see it – get specific about what you want to attract into your life and define prosperity for yourself
* How to use the breakout technique to undo any remaining blocks
* How to create a prosperity list
* How to feel it – make sure you create prosperity, not just money

Visualize with clarity

The week after I turned 30, I went overseas to earn my fortune. Well, actually, I did not want a fortune, but I did have a very specific amount of money in mind. It was not an arbitrary sum. I came up with this particular amount because it was the general cost of the sort of home in which I visualized myself living. It was far more than I could have afforded to spend up to this point, and so for me it symbolized wealth and prosperity. I had not heard of the Law of Attraction (see page 11), but I did believe that it was possible to create one's own future.

I am not certain that I really knew what I was going to do with the money, but in the back of my mind I felt that this was the amount of money that would liberate me. I would be able to buy a property, then do a job I really wanted to do. Of course, I could have just gone to do the job I wanted to do and earned the money that way, but my beliefs at that time did not allow this as a possibility.

I was keen to create this money in my first year on the job. I knew that this was perfectly possible because I worked in the financial markets, with their system of bonuses, plus I was working in a very low tax environment. But at the end of the first year my bonus was smaller than

I had hoped. And so, I carried on. Focusing on my end goal got me through the next year and a half, when I received a bigger bonus. I still did not have quite as much in savings as I originally envisaged, but I decided to quit my job and return to England anyway. As I was packing up, I received a letter from my employer. While I had been abroad, I had paid into some sort of insurance fund. Leaving the country meant that I was entitled to a rebate, and the amount took my total savings to exactly the sum of money I had wanted to create. So, had my goal worked? Well, yes and no. I did end up with exactly the amount of money I had been seeking, but I really had not thought things through in the right way. You see, money really is just a means to an end, not the end in itself. When I arrived back in the United Kingdom, I found exactly the place I wanted to buy, almost identical to the home that had inspired me to begin with, but because I had visualized the money, rather than owning the home outright, what I found was that the cost of property had boomed while I had been away.

The moral of the story — one I have paid attention to ever since — is to visualize what you want to have as the result of money, not just the amount of money that you think you will need to achieve this. In other words, if property prices move as you are in the middle of attracting the money you want in order to buy a property, be sure that your intention to attract the property stands ahead of your

> ## Visualize the result of money, not just the amount of money that you think you will need.

intention to attract whatever money you think it will take to buy it.

The Law of Attraction really does work, and it is specific, so you need to be as clear as you can be about what you want. In this chapter you will be asked to think about your dreams for the future and to break them down into individual intentions or goals. (Use of the word 'intention' here is deliberate because it implies that it is something that you have decided to do; the words 'goal' and 'cosmic order' can also be used interchangeably.)

The power of intentions

One of the most famous stories about attracting wealth is the story of the martial arts genius Bruce Lee. Growing up in Hong Kong, Bruce Lee had a vision of what he wanted to achieve. He was apparently very much influenced by one of the great writers about money and the Law of Attraction, Napoleon Hill, author of *Think and Grow Rich*, which was originally published in 1937. Hill had studied the world's richest men and worked out that they all had a clear way in which they went about attracting wealth — what we now think of as the Law of Attraction method. These wealthy, powerful men all knew exactly the amount of money they wanted to create, with a date attached by when they wanted it. They knew what they would do with it once they had it, and they kept their focus on that sum of money. What's more, each one of them had a plan to get it, even though that plan was, of course, subject to change according to the circumstances encountered. Every wealthy man whom Hill interviewed took action to help their dreams manifest on the material level.

They did not just sit there waiting for wealth to hit them; they took definite steps to make things happen, so that they could meet their own deadlines for achieving wealth.

Bruce Lee did become enormously successful, with a big 'but'... When he died it was found that he had written out an exact goal — to achieve world fame by 1970 and by 1980 to have ten million dollars. He had also written of his intention to be the 'highest paid Oriental superstar in the United States'. Did he achieve his goals? Yes, in part, but at a price. Fame brought with it its own excesses, including stress, and he died young – in 1973 at the age of 32. From his story we can draw two conclusions. Firstly, that Napoleon Hill's advice works and, secondly, how important it is to make sure that you are truly ready in your beliefs to attract wealth in a happy way, otherwise you will attract money without joy.

The first steps to deciding your future

It is vital to make sure that you are really certain about the future you intend to manifest. So, before you think about how much money you want to manifest, think first about your life as a whole. It cannot be stressed enough how crucial it is that you truly understand that it will do you no good at all to create a certain sum of money if you do not know what to do with it, or if you use it in a way that harms you or others. This is why it is important to take the time to think first about what you love doing in life; only after having done this should you consider the amount of money you may need to manifest it.

That being said, considerable personal and professional experimentation has shown me that it can help many people to focus effectively if they also have a specific sum of money in mind that they want to manifest (as long as they are really clear about why this is essential to their other plans). Manifesting money to make other goals happen will help you to build your belief that the Law of Attraction can and does work for you. If, on the other hand, you are already very tuned into your beliefs

> It is vital to make sure that you are certain about the future you intend to manifest.

about your ability to manifest, you may not need this 'means' goal, but instead can simply focus on the end goal – what you are going to use the money for will then come to you. I used to suggest to people that they do this straight away, and indeed this may be the best way for you – that is, form your intention minus the money part – but this does not work for everyone immediately if their beliefs need time and evidence to change.

What do you love doing?

Prosperity is about using money to create a better life — a life in which you can do what you love to do.

What are you passionate about? What do you long to free yourself up to do?

My choices are not going to be your choices. It is really important that you are true to yourself, and your vision comes from you rather than from outside influences, because it is only you who will live your life.

Think about the hobbies and interests you have. Are you a passionate quilt-maker who wants to travel the world to study quilt making, or do you want to create a

> They key is to get really clear and think through what a prosperous life would feel like.

life where you free up time every night to go dancing? Perhaps looking after children or animals makes you happy. Perhaps you would be happiest running your own international business or becoming a top lawyer. The following exercise will help you to work out both the what and the why of what makes you happy.

Take the time to jot down some of the things that make you happy — and remember to make this list all about you and not about other people's or society's expectations.

What?

What do you really enjoy doing with your life? What do you want to create the freedom to do? These are such simple questions to ask, but so vital to any kind of intention work. Write down as much as possible.

Why?

Look at what you have written. Next to each response write down some reasons why this particular thing is so important for you to have in your life. If you decide that it is a 'nice-to-have' rather than a 'must-have', ask yourself the hard questions about whether you feel passionate enough about it to manifest it in your life. Think about what having this will add to your life. What positive feelings will it bring you? What will you need to do to create a balance in your life? What will make you feel good? Are there any activities here that you could use as a source of income?

Next, check the following. If you had all this, would you feel passionate about your life? Anything missing? What are the highest priorities? Are there some that would bring more joy to your life than others?

The key is to get really clear and to think through what a prosperous list would look like and feel like. One of the ways to test that you are on the right track is to sit back and look at what you have written. How does it make you feel? If you experience an excited or happy feeling rising in your body, you are definitely on the right track.

Why is this important?

Experience shows me that every time I have truly needed money for a purpose that is central either to my survival or my general wellbeing or life purpose, the money has appeared, whether in the form of a banknote on the pavement or in the guise of a sudden gift of work from a client. Create the need for money, rather than making it an end in itself, and money will come to you.

Know why you want the money, and what you are going to use it for immediately or in the long term. There is no point pretending to yourself that you are going to use it to start a charity for impoverished children if you actually want it to buy yourself a flashy car and lots of jewellery. The universe does not work as your moral compass in this way. It is not going to discriminate against you for wanting to have nice things in your life. The only dreams

that backfire on us are ones that are not fully thought through. If you want a flashy car and jewellery, then think about how the rest of your life will change as a result.

Think about how this will impact others. Think about what kind of person you will become as a result. The same applies if you want money to help impoverished children. It may look like the more virtuous goal on the surface, but who knows what lives you may touch in positive ways by chasing a more material

> The only dreams that backfire on us are ones that are not fully thought through.

dream? Many of the richest people on the planet end up accidentally or on purpose helping many, many people along the way.

(By the way, if you take issue with the last statement, as I probably did once upon a time, then it is worth thinking about whether you have any negative beliefs about wealth being somehow immoral.)

Exercise

Make a prosperity list

Start to break down your vision into specific intentions by creating a prosperity list out of your initial brainstorm (see pages 38–43). Think about the life you intend to live and break down your desires into a bigger list. Expand each entry as much as possible, embellishing the details and being more specific with your 'wants'.

As an example, below is a basic starting list that Tania compiled to get her creative juices going. She then expanded this considerably because she began to let herself dream that she could have all the things that were lacking in her life at that moment.

For Tania, having a life of prosperity means:

* Paying all her bills with money to spare every month.

* Going on holiday and travelling business class.

* Owning her own home, which she live in with her family.

* Eating out three times a week.

* Being able to pay for gifts for her husband and children.

* Having a new car – it is a silver Mini.

* Knowing she has a great retirement plan and that she can have a luxurious retirement.

* Having enough savings to pay for her children's education outright, while still keeping plenty of savings to afford the way of life she enjoys at present.

* Shopping at Harrods in London and buying designer clothes, so that she always looks polished in her job.

* Buying ten or more friends a delicious meal with Champagne at a top restaurant for Christmas, so that they can celebrate and feel good about the year.

* Making generous cash donations to charity.

* Treating herself to top gyms, massages, a personal trainer, a secretary, an agent and a top dance class.

* Having her whole home renovated and redecorated.

Have a go and get some starting thoughts about what you want by making your own prosperity list.

Once you have made your initial list, do not just leave it there. Keep expanding it, so that it become as detailed as possible, then work out why you want all these things in your life. What will they add to your life?

Why not wanting something brings it to you

Here is a trap many of us fall into. Instead of spending our time thinking about how to create a particular future we do want, we spend our time contemplating how we are going to avoid all those things we do not want.

If you are not feeling particularly happy or if you have a chequered history when it comes to money, this is an especially easy trap to fall into. How many times do you catch yourself doing the 'don't wants'? Here are a few common ones:

* I don't want to be poor.
* I don't want to be stuck in a job I hate because I need to earn enough money to pay the bills.
* My goal is to make sure that I am never in debt again and never unhappy again or lonely, or anything else I don't want.

The universe gets a picture from you of a poor, unhappy person and probably gets a burst of strong emotion attached to it as well. The thought form is so strong that the universe receives the image loud and clear. Being a perfectly responsive universe, it does its best to create the intention it has seen and felt for you. The result is, yes, you do create more being in debt, being unhappy and lonely and everything else bundled in.

When you catch yourself expressing a 'don't want', think about how you could turn it into a 'want' statement instead. For example:

* I want to be rich.
* I want to have a fulfilling job that I love where I always have enough money to pay the bills.
* My goal is to make sure I always have money and am happy and surrounded by friends every day.

Turn your 'wants' to 'whens'

One of the common mistakes that people make is to think that if they want something enough it will happen. Well, you know what? I would like to be in the next big Hollywood movie, but it is not going to happen, partly because I do not believe it is, but also because I have not made it into a 'when'.

Having something you want to happen in your life is very different from having the intention that it will happen. A want can stay as a want. As the White Queen says to Alice in *Through the Looking Glass*: 'The rule is, jam tomorrow and jam yesterday, but never jam today.' A want keeps your future in the 'jam tomorrow' category and never lets you eat it today. To make it jam today, see it and feel it as if it is in your present, happening to you. The universe feels it, too, and begins to create it for you.

Your prosperity list is a starting point (see page 144). It gets what you want out into the open. You still need to take another step after this, which is to turn these wants into goals or clearly stated intentions in your mind (or, even better, into real hard copy on paper or on the computer).

Blocks to brainstorming

Is your past the prison warden of your future? If you look at a person's past, you will find many clues about their future. This was said to me once, and I really did not want to believe it. Are we really victims of our past? Well, the conclusion that I have come to is that you can be, but you do not have to be. Many people do find it difficult to decide their futures for themselves because of their beliefs, including a belief that they do not have the 'right' to change. If you have any lack beliefs (see pages 14–16) left from the past, your future is going to be highly predictable: It will be a continuation of your past.

Some people find it easy to dream of a different future. Others cannot come up with anything very much. The latter type of person will say,

'I cannot see anything.' It is true. They cannot see any pictures of their future because their unconscious thoughts remain so focused still on lack and poverty beliefs (see pages 14–16). When the reason this is happening is examined, it always turns out that

> If you have any lack beliefs left, your future is highly predictable: it will be a continuation of your past.

there is a mental/emotional block of some kind. This may have resulted from a past experience that has fed an unconscious belief that it is not OK to create a future of their dreams. It sometimes has come from a group or society belief about it not being OK for anyone to have a prosperous future or earn money and enjoy earning it.

Lack beliefs really are deeply ingrained in many of our lives. It is not surprising, really, when you consider how many wars and famines, and other difficult circumstances humanity has been through over the centuries. This group 'thought form' is still present unconsciously in many families because of family history. In addition, if you have been doing a job you have really hated for a long time, you may not find it easy to separate yourself from the 'you' who is unhappy and, in that career, now. You need to be able to step away from your dissatisfied self-enough to believe in different possibilities for your future.

If you cannot get your dreams out into the light, there are some things that you can do to lift yourself out of your everyday thinking. Go back to the introduction and look at your beliefs in more detail. Work with your spiritual guides and the

> If you cannot get your dreams out into the light, there are some things you can do to lift yourself out of your everyday thinking.

prosperity rituals found in the next few chapters. There are also two techniques opposite and on page 150 that are very effective.

Prosperity breakout

* **Step 1:** Sit down somewhere quiet with your eyes closed. Imagine that you are floating out high above your everyday life. You can see yourself in your life down below.

* **Step 2:** Imagine going higher and higher into the air, so that the you below is just a tiny person from the vantage point of the you looking down. You can see all of your life – the past, present and future – spread out below you.

* **Step 3:** Imagine that you are a very powerful being. In this position you have the power to change anything in the timeline below you. Notice how at the moment there is a direct link between what has happened in the past to what will happen in the future. The past contains all your different memories and beliefs. You may even see the past going back farther than this current lifetime into past lives or into the lives of your parents and grandparents and other ancestors. Notice where on your timeline there has been an event or incident that has changed the patterns of thoughts, conscious and unconscious, and therefore what has been attracted into your life when it comes to prosperity, wealth or money issues.

Step 4: You have a choice to change your destiny. You can change anything on this timeline. Open up the top of your head (the crown chakra, see page 43). Imagine that the healing, loving light of the universe is flowing through you and out through your heart down to the timeline below. Breathe deeply and, as you exhale and release the breath, imagine that it is full of light energy. See the energy repair any fractured points on the timeline that need to be sent love and healing. Imagine that, as you do this, your future is changing as a result. Notice how your future timeline changes. Perhaps it changes colour or direction, or even width. From your vantage point, you may observe future events in your timeline. Let the loving light fill your future, so that your future is free to become a future of your dreams. You have broken out from your past and no longer need to be its prisoner. You can make of your future what you will.

Step 5: As you do this, some ideas for your future may spontaneously pop into your mind. You may also go down and take a closer look at your future. Choose a point in your timeline that corresponds to a particular date in the future. What dreams can you see being manifested there? How do you feel

Gain clarity about what you really want to manifest in your life.

about them? If they are not strong enough yet, imagine that you have the power to turn them to dreams of pure gold. Shoot a golden light into the event and change the circumstances of your future into the best and most prosperous they can possibly be.

Step 6: When you have completed this, gently float back down into your body. Take a deep breath to ground yourself and come back into the room by opening your eyes.

Notice how this exercise frees you up to write down your dreams and gain clarity about what you really want to manifest in your life.

Exercise

Lift your vibration

Bringing laughter into your life lifts the vibration of your energy. It shakes off the shackles of your present feelings and frees up your mind to get creative.

Watch some comedy. Read a happy book. Dance to some silly music. Do whatever you need to do to get yourself laughing. The more, the better. Once you have spent time having fun, it is time to get creative:

* Settle down with some coloured pens and paper, and draw a picture of your happy, prosperous future as freely as you would if you were a child.

* Do this in stages if you like. Use a combination of words and pictures and stick them all on a big sheet of paper. Draw your own images and add inspiring pictures you have cut from magazines. See what this sparks off in your imagination over the following few days.

* As your dreams become clearer, start to write them down in more detail.

Live your dreams

Living your dreams is so important to your success in manifesting a prosperous future that I want you to really get into living your dreams before they happen. Take a look at everything you have written down in the exercise on the previous pages. Your future is not set. There are so many possibilities for you to create. Is this the future you really want?

Consider each item on your prosperity list (see page 144) in turn. Now imagine that your life contains each of these. How is it going to affect you? What does it feel like? Do you like the person you have become when you have this item?

Project yourself mentally at least ten years in the future. Twenty is good. The farther into the future we can project ourselves, the easier it is to free ourselves from the constraints of the present.

Are you happy? Are you laughing? If not, what can you add to your dream to make it happy and full of lightness and laughter?

There is no need to rush this process. Be sure that you really break the pattern of your particular past, rather than just come up with a list that is full of 'ought tos' or 'shoulds' — or the same generic list as everyone else's on the planet. You do not need to create the dreams of your friends or of your mother or father or anybody else. Free yourself from the past. Let your imagination take you fully into an entirely new way of living, one that goes beyond all your previous limitations. Mentally explore every corner of your dream life. See yourself getting up in the morning. See yourself with your friends. See yourself being happy. See yourself in the career that will help you to create this wealth and prosperous life. See yourself as successful. See what you are buying with your wealth. Imagine that your home is

> The more detail you can find in your dream, the more you can consolidate it in your mind.

full of beautiful things. See what you are wearing. Imagine what you are doing with your wealth. Notice the activities in which you take part.

The more detail you can find in your dream, the more you can consolidate it in your mind. And the more you live your dreams before they happen, the more successful you will be in manifesting them.

The key to success: feeling

Key to successful manifestation are the pictures you make in your mind's eye of your intentions and also the strength of the feelings you have attached to them. The Law of Attraction works according to thoughts and emotions (see page 11). If you can feel what it will really be like when you have attracted prosperity into your life, you will then get exactly what you have asked for. The more you can feel your future life exactly as if it is really happening to you right now, the more successful you will be at attracting prosperity. This is why it is really important to engage the creative, imaginative part of your mind.

Consider your intentions fully, and really imagine them happening to you as if it is now. Let yourself loose to dream. Use your heart to feel whether something is right or now. Then decide that this will happen and when it will happen. When you do this, you create a future energetic memory in the timeline of your life.

The creative part of the universe does not contain a past, present or future.

In the spirit universe the time is always now. Imagine your future as if it is happening to you right now and the spirit universe will hear your belief. Then, according to the rules of time and space we live by in this part of the universe, your intention will come to you.

You do not need the how

It is a mistake to think that you need to know every step of how you will make this vision become a reality. As long as you commit to making this vision happen and take some first steps, the universe will help you along with a little bit or a lot of luck.

You can, if you like, break down a vision for you in, say, ten years' time into different intentions/goals that act as steppingstones along the way. One way to do this is to imagine in your mind that you are already in your life in ten years' time. Now look back from that vantage point in the future toward now — the point from where your journey is beginning.

As you look along the path that has taken you from now to the future, notice, if you wish, things that happened along the way that gave you cause for celebration. These things may or may not actually happen. By seeing one possible route or the many possible routes to your dreams, you allow your unconscious trust that you will definitely realize your dreams to grow, and as it grows, your manifestation power is also boosted.

Exercise

Create your intention list

Your next step to manifesting your vision is to write down your goals/intentions (all of them!) Remember to:

* Give the universe a clear message about how you intend your life to be.

* Take any negatives out of your prosperity lists, for example, don't list what you don't want.

* Focus intently on each area of your life where you have a clear goal by writing an intention statement for each item on your prosperity list as laid out below.

Create intentions for five, ten and twenty years. Some of these intentions will be about what you want to use your wealth for. Some may include a specific amount of money. The key is to remember that money intentions work best not when you are feeling desperate – because then you are vibrating 'lack' thoughts to the universe – but when you are happy and joyful about how you will spend your money.

✳

The rules of intention statements

* Write your intention in the present tense as if it is happening to you right now (this way you feel your intention becoming real). SEE it, FEEL it, HEAR it. Create a positive emotional connection to it.

* Be specific about WHAT you want.

* Be clear WHY you want this – your intention must be personally compelling for it to have sufficient energetic 'charge' to manifest.

* Be clear WHEN you want this. This helps you to focus clearly on what you will create.

* Be clear that having this in your life will be good – for you and for everyone else who might be impacted by it.

* Decide what you are going to DO to make this happen as a FIRST STEP even if the universe may eventually give it to you in another way.

* WRITE DOWN YOUR INTENTION. This ensures that you commit to your intention.

Imagine that one of your intentions is to manifest savings of a specific amount of money within two years. The reason that you want this is for a deposit on a property. You are clear in your mind that having a property will free you up to do other things you want in your life. You see yourself and feel yourself living happily in the property with your family. You imagine that you have beautiful furniture and a joyous life there. You have thought this intention through, including the impact on other parts of your life of paying an ongoing mortgage. The first actions you intend to take toward this are to apply for a new job and to start regular payments into a savings account. You write down a statement like the one on the opposite page.

Your intention statement

It is 16 March 2030. I have my savings account balance written down in front of me. It shows that I have 'x' amount in my bank account, which has come to me over the period up to this point.

Important: Make sure as you look at this statement that you have a clear picture of it, as if this imagined scene is happening now. Then look at the picture from another angle seeing yourself looking at your bank balance. This should appear as though you are playing back a scene in a movie. Next, decide what part you are going to play in creating this scenario, by writing down at least

> Say thank you in advance to the universe for what it is about to bring into your life.

one first step towards your goal. This should be a step that you intend to make immediately.

My first step is to open a savings account.

Say thank you

Remember to say thank you in advance to the universe for what it is about to bring into your life. Thanks, should always be said because, in one part of the universe, this change has already been created — we just can't see it yet. Every time you create a clear picture and feel it as if it is real, you create a future memory, as real in the universe as a past memory.

Thank you for this already having happened in the best way and to the highest good of all concerned.

The ideal date

It definitely helps to put dates to intentions. Putting in place a time frame works to make the intentions more real — with one caveat. It is far better to write down long-term intentions than short-term goals. There is a danger in putting down dates that are too near the present.

The focus you keep on your intention is best if it is a 'soft' intention — in other words, so that you remember the date you have set without becoming obsessed or needy of the intention manifesting by that date. Constantly thinking about the date, you have set makes you like a cake-watching cook — opening up the oven door every five minutes to check whether your cake is really baking or not. The result with a cake is that it collapses from too much attention. It is the same with your goals. If you keep rechecking them, you create the vibration of doubt, and doubt delays the manifestation of the goal.

Summary

Take the time to decide what you want. What is your vision of a happy, prosperous life? Decide how much money you want. Know why you want this amount. What are you going to use it for?

Next, question yourself. Why is this important? This will clarify your dreams and help you to decide what you are going to devote your efforts toward achieving.

Take what you have brainstormed and turn it into a clear vision and a list of goals/intentions. Make sure that you have worded these positively and have fully imagined what your life will feel like when you have it.

Now let go and trust that these intentions are already a future memory in the creative brain of the universe. They already exist and are just waiting to come into your life. Stay positive, making sure that your beliefs support your intention to receive this future prosperity.

3: Play Your Part

'A bank book makes good reading –
better than some novels.'

Entertainer Harry Lauder

This is a very practical chapter. Creating your future is
teamwork. The universe will help you if you play your part and
help to co-create your future. If you just sit there and wait for
something to happen, the likelihood is that it will not. If you take
the initiative to create the circumstances that you want in your
life, you will be rewarded as the universe supports you by
bringing you the people and opportunities to take inspired
action. As you take action it is important to ensure that your
beliefs continue to support what you want to achieve.

Keep developing your loving relationship with the idea of
prosperity and business.

In this chapter you will learn:
* How to play your part in co-creating your future
* How the universe rewards personal responsibility
* How to stay receptive to signals from the universe
* How to continue developing your loving relationship
  with wealth

The gods help those who help themselves

It is true that you do not ever need to know every step of how you are going to achieve your goals, but you do have to keep taking actions and seizing opportunities that come your way. The universe does not help us if we do nothing — only if it sees us taking action toward our goals. It is simply an extension of the premise of giving and receiving. If you expect something to come to meet you, you must make the effort to go to meet it. As the old adage goes, the gods help those who help themselves. People really do help to create their own luck.

The way this works always reminds me of an old joke: Bob is desperate for money. He prays to God: 'I will do my best to become more religious and practise everyday if

> ## The universe does not help us if we do nothing.

you can only help me to win the lottery.' He waits by the TV the next day to check his numbers. Not one of his numbers comes up.

Bob is now really desperate. He falls onto his knees and begs, 'God, please help me. If I don't win the lottery tonight, then it is all over. I will go bankrupt and the bailiffs will

be at my door. Help me, please.' He watches the lottery numbers again. Nothing. Not even one of his numbers has come up.

A week later Bob prays again, sobbing to God, 'God, you must help me. This is absolutely my last chance. My wife says she will leave me and take the kids. I will lose my house and everything in it. I am begging you, Lord, please help me to win the lottery.'

Suddenly there is a clap of mighty thunder. The clouds part and a deep voice is heard from the heavens.

'Bob. Meet me halfway here. Go and buy a lottery ticket!'

Here's another joke. Not about money this time, but still the same idea — that we must play our part in what happens to us: A priest was in his church giving a sermon when suddenly it began to rain. It rained and rained, and soon the whole place was flooded. The people started to leave the church because the water was already up to their ankles. The priest kept on preaching while everyone else left. One of the congregation called out to him, 'Sir, you must leave. You will be caught in the floods.'

'Don't worry about me,' answered the priest, smiling happily. 'God will save me.'

Now everyone had left and the water was up to the priest's knees. One of the people of the town drove past in a car and saw the priest standing there through the open door of the church. 'I can help you,' he said to the priest.

'No need, no need,' waved the priest happily. 'God will save me.'

The waters continued to rise. A man in a boat rowed past the church. 'Hey. Swim here and I can help you. You are going to drown,' he called to the priest.

'No, I'm fine,' smiled the priest. 'God will save me.'

The floodwaters rose higher and higher. The priest started to climb onto the roof of the church. At that moment a man in a rescue helicopter flew by and saw the priest there. 'Quick,' he called out. 'Come here before you drown and I will rescue you.'

'I am OK,' the priest said once more. 'Don't bother about me. The Lord will save me.' The pilot tried to persuade him to leave the church, but the priest refused to get onto the helicopter. 'Leave me. God will help me.' Eventually the helicopter flew away.

The waters rose and rose, and sadly the priest was swept into the waters and drowned. The next thing he knew, he was in heaven. The first person he saw was God.

'God, why didn't you save me?' asked the priest. 'Wasn't I a good man?

Didn't I pray and pray? Yet you deserted me.'

God replied, 'I sent you a car and a boat and a helicopter. What else did you want me to do?'

Take responsibility for yourself and your future

The wealthy people I have met, those who have held on to their wealth, all have one thing in common. They know that if they lost their wealth, they would make sure that they became wealthy again. How? They did not know at that point. It did not matter really. They simply knew that because they took responsibility for creating wealth the first time around that they could do it again, rather than just rely on luck bringing it to them. This wealth-keeping mindset is shared not only by self-made millionaires and wealthy professionals, but also by many people I know who have inherited wealth. Those lucky individuals divide into two camps: those who just go and spend their inheritance and those who use the money to invest wisely, carrying the wealth forward to the next generation. All of the prosperous individuals I have met around the world have an unshakeable faith that they will create wealth and prosperity by taking action and having a clear vision of their future. They are not swayed by the doubts of those who sit and wait for luck to hit them.

Taking action and taking responsibility are part of a prosperous mindset. This chapter will show you some ways that you can reinforce your abundance and prosperity beliefs through action. This in turn will help the universe to pull your intention into creation.

Take inspired action

You never know exactly how the universe will make your intention manifest, but the good thing is that you do not need to know every single thing that you are going to do to make your intention manifest. The universe will help you.

What is always clear, however, is that the universe rewards action and personal responsibility. Manifesting anything is a joint project between you and the universe. What part will you play in creating the future you want? This is something that a lot of people do not like to dwell on because they hope that, if they do nothing toward realizing their intentions, they will happen anyway. Remember that this is a universe of flow. By giving a service in return for the intention you manifest, the universe brings that intention to you for realization.

You have already outlined in your intention statement (see page 153) some action or service you going to perform. Now it is time to think a little bit more about how you are going to stay on track, focusing on

The universe rewards action and personal responsibility.

the end goal. Think of every practical action that you take toward your intentions as an investment.

For example, let us take the sample intention in the last chapter (see page 155). It is very clear. You need to get a specific amount of money together within two years for a down payment on a property. How are you going to do this? Well, you know the work you want to do and you have started saving; however, in your mind you cannot see that this is going to be enough. What do you do next?

You keep your focus on the end prize, and let the universe guide you — by bringing you opportunities to take action, or what I call 'inspired actions'. These opportunities may appear mundane — well, that is because they are. But they have come your way only because of the thoughts and intentions you have put out to the universe. The key is taking personal responsibility for making your intentions happen, which helps you to get creative and notice the opportunities that come your way.

Take care of the money you have already

Here is a good starting point for everyone. Although prosperity is about more than just money, you do need to have a good relationship with your existing money. If this is not the case, take steps to change the situation — it is all part of being grateful for what you have already received.

When you create prosperity there is one big change that is inevitable. You will be much richer than you are now. Many rich people pay others to advise them what to do with their wealth. Others pay accountants and bookkeepers to keep an eye on their current cash

> They key is taking personal responsibility for making your intentions happen.

flow. That is all very well, but however rich you are, you need to keep an eye on your wealth and guide those who help you. After

all, there have been some amazing cases of even the fabulously wealthy overspending and going into debt, even going bankrupt. I could never understand how this happened when I was younger, but it is much clearer to me now, having observed the spending patterns of different people over the years. If you do not stay in charge of the basic details of your finances, it is easy to get carried away with buying things you do not need or to make bad investments — or to let other people take advantage of you.

Do the wealthy throw their money around? Actually, no. Surveys show that the truly wealthy tend to live well within their means. They are not all that fussed about showing off their high status at the expense of wealth. Warren Buffett, one of the most successful investors in the world, is a classic example. He still lives in a relatively modest home despite enormous financial success.

Reverse previous bad management

Does neglect pay a part in your financial management? Do you feel trapped by money?

Break any bad financial habits that you have. If you are stuck in a cycle of overdrafts or credit-card debt while earning at least an average salary, it is within your power to make a change. Take a big breath. Sit down and write down what you can do to cut out unnecessary spending. Getting to grips with the details will prevent you from

> # Getting to grips with the details will prevent you sabotaging the intentions you have set.

creating more lack thinking (see page 14) and sabotaging the intentions you have set. It breaks the cycle of bad financial decision-making. Write out everyone you owe, such as credit-card or store-card companies, and set an intention/goal with a date by when you will have cleared this debt. Follow the structure of the intention example in the previous chapter (see page 153–155).

Doing this may involve a life change. Perhaps you will need to rent out a spare room, take on some extra work or give up some luxuries. If it does, realize that the universe will support you.

Invest in your future

If you talk to millionaires, one thing many of them have in common is that they invest for the future. They will happily sacrifice rewards in the present for rewards in the future. This is because they believe absolutely in their ability to create their visions.

Even if they do not start with much business or financial know-how, they make sure to acquire it by paying attention. Successful accumulators of wealth research investments. They find out ways to increase their savings income and earn money not just from their salaries, but also as they sleep — from their investments. It helps to remember the following:

* When in doubt, take an action toward your intention. Sitting there doing nothing shows the universe that you are not playing your part. Do not just try to do something; stand up and do whatever you think you have the resources to do right now. You will be rewarded for taking responsibility.

* Budget your money and budget your time to keep your life in balance. Plan your income and expenses ahead. Financial independence will be your reward.

* Know what you earn – before and after tax. Know how much

money you have available for essentials and how much for luxuries. Is there anything you do not need now that could be better used as savings or for investing toward the future?

* Start up a regular savings account. On a very basic level, hopefully you are going to get paid interest on what is in there. Already you are accumulating wealth.

Love your money

The key to creating wealth and prosperity is to learn to love thinking about what you are going to do with your money.

You need to start to develop a love relationship with investments. You do not have to have a lot of money to begin with; all savings can begin on a shoestring. Begin by developing a good relationship with the idea or energy of money. This ensures that you do not lapse back into lack beliefs (see page 14) because you will feel on top of things. Knowing that you know as much (or more) about money as everybody else helps you to feel that you can be prosperous because it is in your hands.

Having worked in the international financial markets means that I am not afraid of reading about money and business, but many of my friends — and especially my friends who label themselves as 'spiritual' — are very fearful of the idea of money. This is not true in all societies, but nonetheless there are millions of people around the world who are not entirely comfortable with the idea of money. I do understand this. Before I got my first job working with money, I had never picked up a business newspaper in my life. Unlike many of my colleagues, I had not studied economics or business or finance. I certainly could not read a set of accounts, and I had only a very

> Feel better and you will be in control of your prosperity creation.

vague idea what a stock was or a bond was. I had to learn on the job very quickly. But I can tell you, it is possible for anyone to learn the basics of how money works — and you will feel much better for it. Feel better and you will be in control of your prosperity creation.

Keep track of the money

Do not just do your accounts once at the end of the financial year. Keep track of how near you are to realizing your goals. This takes commitment, but it also keeps you focused on the end reward. Remember what you focus on is what you get — it is a basic part of the Law of Attraction (see page 11).

If you are someone who sticks everything in a drawer hoping it will go away, stop it! Get all your receipts and money-related papers out and take a good hard look at them. By keeping track of your finances, you will be able to see when you take a wrong turning and pull yourself back. You will notice if you are spending too much or

> # Remember, what you focus on is what you get.

perhaps earning but not enjoying your life or perpetuating any other past poor prosperity habits. It is fascinating looking at spending and earning. Do you know how much you spend on coffees during a year or how much interest you earn from your savings? Know where you are now, and you will become clearer on where to make changes.

Reward

Remember your intention is to create financial success in a way that creates more joy in your life. If it helps, give yourself rewards for each small milestone you reach on the

way. For example, if your intention is to create, say, £40,000 or $65,000 in two years, and you save £2,000 or $3,250 toward this, tell yourself good things for having done this. Not only will this make you feel good, but the positive feelings will energize your intentions as well, pulling in the positive power of the universe to help you. Our intentions are often many years ahead, so it is important to keep yourself positive and feeling good for the long haul, not just the short sprint.

Choose an appropriate way to monitor and reward yourself as you work toward your intentions/goals:

* Perhaps you could create ten percent reward point, or maybe a milestone marking when you are one-third toward your goal.

* Keep a spreadsheet so that you can see how far you have come.

* Write down your 'wins' on a piece of paper and stick it on your wall to remind you of your progress.

* Keep a calendar and, when you have done something toward one of your intentions, draw a big cross through that day. You will be able to see at a quick, satisfying glance just how far you have come in the course of a year.

Examine your wealth-creating skills

Wealthy people are clever enough to realize that attaining goals is often a team effort. Self-made millionaires, in particular, tend to be independent-minded people. They draw in money by focusing on providing a service they are passionate about and creating an expertise in that area. At the same time they find people to support them in areas in which they are weaker.

This is something I would encourage you to do. If in doubt, just ask the universe to bring the right person to you who will help you with X or Y. Keep a look out – the universe will give you an opportunity for action.

At the same time, you can increase your ability to earn. Be really clear with yourself what your skills are. If you are not sure, ask people who know you in a personal and professional context. Do not limit yourself to just asking people in one area of your life because not everybody knows us in the same way. Our early careers do not always give us the scope to show off all our talents.

If you are lacking skills, get ready to educate yourself – not just about money, but also in any field you love. I was brought up to think of a life in a profession, such as law, or in a traditional business as the only route to future prosperity. This is not the case any longer, especially with the rise of the Web and the interconnectedness of everyone around the globe. There is always a skill that someone somewhere needs and someone somewhere else can fulfil. Examine your hobbies and interests for opportunities to create wealth. After all, who would have thought that a company such as eBay could be a route to commercial success for many people sitting in their own homes.

Let your passion lead you closer to prosperity

Be clear about your passions as well as your skills. If you like doing something, you will put way more effort into it but most importantly you will feel good, and as we know, the Law of Attraction works on feelings. By the way, do not worry if finding work you love and can dedicate yourself to one hundred percent to takes a while to explore. Just keep your eye on the end goal of wealth plus joy.

Apparently, the average millionaire does not find his or her real flow until reaching their mid-40s. You may or may not intend to be a millionaire, but you can still relax and take your time. If you are not sure what would be perfect for you, keep working hard at whatever you can do to take you nearer to the intentions you have written down

> **If you feel that you are on the right track, you are likely to keep taking action towards what you want.**

(see page 153). If you feel that you are on the right track, you are likely to keep taking action towards what you want. This will reinforce your beliefs that you can attract prosperity and having these ideas of abundance will keep you attracting the life you want.

Find a mentor

Here is another thing that wealthy people do. They keep learning. They surround themselves with people who can teach them what they need to know. Take a look at someone's friends and you will learn a lot about them. If you cannot find a person in your immediate circle who can teach you, find a virtual mentor. Learn from people you read about or watch on screen.

Spiritual traditions practised around the planet have long passed on wisdom from teacher to student as a natural way of learning over a lifetime. You do not need to be born knowing everything in one go. Life is, as it is always said to be, a journey of discovery. You will gain the knowledge you need to gain as you go along. If you have a focus – your prosperity intention – for what you need to learn, then this can speed things up.

Be receptive

The most important thing you can do to attract money toward you is to be clear about what you want. If you are really clear about what your life will be like when you have attracted money, and know why that matters to you, the universe is going to come along with a load of happy surprises in the way you achieve your intention. You can then take action.

Be receptive. Keep an eye out for opportunities. Listen to what people say to you. Seize the networking opportunity or job opening you are offered. Perhaps one day you may get an e-mail out of the blue offering you the chance to train in a new area or to volunteer for the day. Out of this chance comes an encounter with an important businessperson. Twenty years later you have built a business together with a turnover in the millions. Have you ever found that people come back into your life, or into your life for the first time, and open doors for you out of the blue? Some people would call this the power of networking. I think of it also as the universe's way of helping us out when we are moving toward an intention.

These calls from the universe may seem mundane and not 'magic' enough to be 'gifts' as such. The thing is, the universe does not put a big label on an opportunity – 'This is an opportunity you must take' or 'This is the one you created when you wrote your vision down on that bit of paper' – but it does throw us calls to action out of the blue. If we are not receptive to them, they go away. If we are, it speeds up our progress toward our intentions.

Developing a good relationship with money

The actions below are ways for you to reinforce positive beliefs about money and to develop a better relationship with the spirit of money. I used to hate bills coming in. I hated doing my accounts or keeping a close eye on how much money I had in my bank account. I did all these necessary things, but without pleasure and sometimes with a certain amount of fear.

It will really help you to manifest more money if you can develop a good relationship with the spirit, or energy, of money. If you are still unsure or ambivalent about your relationship with money, here are some ways in which you can change the energy of your thoughts about it. They are all very practical, and they will reinforce abundance beliefs (see page 14).

Pay your bills with joy

Let's start with bills. How many of us fear that window-faced envelope dropping through the door, the official-looking one with the name of the tax office on the outside? What would it be like if you could free yourself up from worrying about opening your bills and seeing what is inside? I have always made myself rip them open as quickly as possible, even when I did not have much money. It is the sticking plaster principle: get it off quick and

> Free yourself up from worrying about opening your bills.

it will hurt less. I have many friends who are much more afraid than me, and let their bills fester in their envelopes, unopened in a drawer.

If this is you, why not start making your bill opening and paying into rituals of thanks to the spirit of money. If you feel bad every time you are about to send a cheque off to pay a bill, you are not showing much trust that an abundant flow will come to you. If you pay with joy, you are going to switch on the flow of abundance and attract it toward you.

A bill is a gift of trust. You have already received a service or will receive a service in return for this sum of money. It is a simple energy exchange based on good faith and trust. Paying your bills joyfully is an expression of thanks for the goodwill of the service provider and therefore to the universe, which has enabled this energetic exchange.

Changing your prosperity energy

For a month, get to know the business pages of the newspaper. Make sure that you read them every day; alternatively, read the business news online. If you do not understand the terminology, buy a book or check it out on the Web. Read up about your local economy and the world economy. Do you understand what inflation is? Do you know what is meant by a credit crunch or a recession? If not, do a little studying.

As you do this each day, focus on how you feel. This is a good way to discover any limiting beliefs or negative feelings that you have about money that may be lurking around. Really focus in. After you have read around for a few days, pick one subject.

If negative thoughts or emotions emerge, dissolve them away.

For example, how about picking the idea of the stock market. Hold the image you have of the stock market in your mind. Really examine it. How do you feel in relation to this concept?

Where are you feeling these feelings? You may notice movement, or warmth or cold, or another sensation in a particular part of your body. Do you perhaps associate particular sounds or even tastes or smells with the term?

How do you feel toward the energy of this idea associated with money?

Do any particular thoughts emerge? Take careful note of them.

If any negative thoughts or emotions emerge, dissolve them away. You can do this energetically by imagining that you are opening up the top of your head – the crown chakra (see page 43) – and letting in the highest universal energy, which is the energy of love and light and creative force. Now let that light flow down through your body and out through your heart, dissolving away all the negative beliefs and feelings. See them leave. Feel your emotions turn as you love the idea of, in this example, the stock market. Then say the words 'I love …,' followed by whatever the idea is. It gets easier the more you do it.

Do not worry if this feels a little strange or artificial at first. Learning any new habit takes practice. Love is the highest force in the universe, and by channelling it through you again and again toward any idea with which you have an uneasy or unclear relationship, you can create an entirely new and positive relationship in its stead.

Take account of the group mind

As discussed on page 16, group beliefs are very powerful. If you believe something, there is always a certain amount of energy going toward it. If millions of people believe something, obviously a lot more energy goes toward this belief. This can work in your favour. If you want to adopt a new, positive mindset, find a group of people who think in this way and, if you are open, you will find it easy to adopt their beliefs. Soon you will find yourself attracting similar luck,

as long as you do not have any other beliefs that are in conflict with this new set of positive or abundant ones.

One example of this was my becoming a member of the international investment community. Despite the fact that I had grown up with very little money, once I was in this new environment, I soon assumed that I could make money because everyone around me did.

Of course, such group beliefs can work the other way as well. In other circumstances than those above, I may have thought that I could not charge a particular amount for a service I provided because I would not question the value of what I did in monetary terms when no one else questioned it either. If the group mind has limiting beliefs and you are an open person, you are going to need to take steps to stay away from this negative energy. I found this out as soon as I left my previous profession and for the first time questioned the value of what I did. The exercise on the following page is a ritual that will help you to get back some power to act outside these limiting beliefs.

Undoing group money and prosperity beliefs

* Think about your current profession. What are some of the commonly held money beliefs found in this profession? Are these useful?

* Now think about the beliefs about money and prosperity in your country as a whole or associated with your politics or peer group. Are these useful?

* Next, think through your life so far. What are the major financial events you have observed? Perhaps you have seen recessions, booms and crashes, including the most recent credit crunch. How have you been affected by these events?

* Have you managed to stay apart from the group mind? Have you bought into group thinking about your ability to create prosperity in these situations? Has this made you more risk-taking? Less risk-taking?

The truth is that you can make money in any circumstances and create a good life in many circumstances, but it is easy to buy into other people's mindsets and be unable to separate your own thinking from the thinking of others. This is a well-known phenomenon in the financial world. When you are young and just starting out, you are untainted by circumstance. Therefore, the investment decisions you take can be quite 'pure' — based on reward, not fear. After you have been through a couple of recessions, on the good side you learn a bit of caution, but on the negative side you may lose your ability to see the opportunities.

Acknowledge your thoughts. Note down any that you think are harming your ability to create prosperity.

Now notice once more how these negative ideas are affecting you on a feeling level. Observe them in your body as emotions with a form to them. Notice any sounds, tastes or smells you associate with them. Take each idea in turn and do this. There is no need to rush; you can do one or two at a time.

If you like, do this in a very meditational way. Sit quietly in a chair or lie down. Close your eyes and really get in touch with the idea — for example, 'recessions harm my ability to earn'. Again, melt away any negative thoughts and feelings using the energy of love (see page 168). With your eyes open or closed, open up your crown chakra and allow the flow of universal energy through to the thoughts and feelings, healing them up with love so that you can let go of them for ever, creating a space that you can now fill with fresh new thoughts of your own that support your intention.

You can also write down an abundance belief (see page 14) concerning this subject in advance and imagine it slotting into the space you have created.

If you have to do this more than once, that is absolutely fine. Practise again and again until you really feel that your emotional reactions have changed and that you can clearly see when and where you have bought into a particular mindset without thinking for yourself first.

Open up your thoughts and feelings, heal them with love so that you can let go of them.

Summary

The key message of this chapter is that you are a co-creator of your life. You work together with the universe to bring about your future. Your role is to define what you want and to take responsibility for making your intention or intentions happen by looking out for opportunities to act.

Be clear what service you are offering the universe in return for prosperity.

Know your skills and your passions. The universe will then support you by inspiring you to take action — bringing the right events into your life that you can take advantage of as you work toward your intention.

Support this co-creation by continuing to develop your positive relationship with money. Keep track of your finances and kick out bad habits. Next, be receptive — the universe may bring the money to you in unexpected ways.

4: Prosperity Rituals

'Men do not attract what they want, but
what they are.'

James Allen, *As a Man Thinketh*

Life is made up of little rituals that reinforce your ordinary life.
We give cards and gifts. We meet up with colleagues or friends.
We cook for those we love. We say prayers. Rituals are strong
ways of expressing belief in what is important to us.

They make us repeat the same thoughts again and again,
reinforcing our conviction that we will attract what we desire.
You can make your own rituals or use existing ones from
different cultures to boost your new beliefs so that you attract
the flow of prosperity into your life.

In this chapter you will learn:
* How to make visual prosperity props, which will
  keep you focused on your intentions
* How to create a symbol of your intention,
  which will draw the energies of it near to you
* The power of using real money for rituals

The rituals help you to change any lingering self-limiting beliefs and boost your trust that you will manifest your intentions, and ultimately the whole vision you have of a prosperous future for yourself. When you repeat the same thought or action again and again, it becomes a habit. Rituals help you to change your inner world — where all your thoughts and emotions are stored — through the power of repetition.

Get clear on your motivation

You can practise any of the rituals within this chapter as they are or, indeed, vary them and make them very personal to you. You can create your own rituals for wealth and prosperity. Whatever rituals you choose to practise, please be very clear about your motivation before carrying them out. Be really honest with yourself. You cannot cheat the universe because the universe picks up on every thought you have, conscious or unconscious.

Wealth rituals have been used for millennia. Religious practitioners prayed to their gods for wealth. Magicians used spells and rituals in order to create wealth for themselves, for others or for countries or kingdoms. They did not always work. One of the big reasons is that many magicians were blocked by the belief that it was wrong to use magic to create wealth. If this is a belief you suspect that you might hold, it is really important to examine the reasons for it and change it, otherwise you will not get the results you want from the rituals that follow in this chapter. One of the best ways to change this belief is to get absolutely clear on the reasons you want wealth. Remember, if you know the why, you will receive the what (see page 70).

Prosperity props

The first ritual is a very simple one: make yourself a prosperity prop.

Prosperity props are a very easy way for you to keep your focus on your vision. Suppose your goal is to attract a radical change in your way of life, involving a new home within a timeline of five years. That is going to take a large amount of money. Fair enough, you can do it. At the same time, you need to be able to sustain your intention over that five-year period. A prosperity prop is a tangible and visual reminder of your prosperity vision. It should make you feel good when you look at it and be specific enough to bring your particular vision into your mind. The right prosperity prop will help you to maintain your trust that you will attract your vision throughout the five years, even if you cannot see any evidence of it manifesting immediately.

Jim Carrey, the Canadian comic and Hollywood movie star, is said to have had his own prosperity prop before he became famous. The story goes that when he was a young and struggling comedian, he was about to give up on his dream of being a success. He sat down by Los Angeles' Mulholland Drive and wrote himself a cheque for $10 million and inscribed on it that it

> Prosperity props are a very easy way to keep your focus on your vision.

was 'for acting services'. He carried the cheque with him as a reminder of what he wanted to achieve. As you know, it worked. By the mid 1990s, Jim Carrey was enormously successful and was able to command fees of millions of dollars per movie.

Making your own prosperity props

Here are some suggestions for prosperity props that are very easy to make and use. You can choose one of the examples listed here or use them as inspiration to tailor a prosperity prop that will most inspire you and help you to keep on track.

1: Write yourself a cheque

Write yourself a cheque for the amount you want to be worth in a few years, time. Postdate it so that it reflects the date by which you want to achieve your intention/goal. For example, write yourself a million-pound or million-dollar cheque for ten years' time. Sign it and address the cheque to yourself.

When you do this, don't just rip a cheque out of your chequebook, fill it in and forget about it. Rituals are powerful because they are acts of concentrated thought and focus. They are about giving you power and are your expression of devotion and trust in the universe. You must treat them with some reverence.

For instance, you can make a prosperity altar in your home by setting aside a space for all your rituals and place your cheque on it. Regularly energize the space around your altar: light candles, pray over it, make offerings of food and pretty objects, or place photographs there of what you intend to use your money for once you have achieved your goal.

2: Property Board

In Decide Your Prosperous Future (see page 138–156), it was suggested that you start drawing or cutting out pictures of what you want, to prompt you to draw up a clear vision of your future (see page 150). This is a technique that works for any kind of goal. Even after you have drawn up your vision of your prosperous future, it is still a good idea to keep a prosperity vision board. You can either make a collage or, preferably, use a corkboard or pinboard. Having a prosperity board is a great way to remind yourself on a daily basis that you are already in the process of creating your prosperity goals.

Collages program your unconscious mind. They help you to create focus and direct your thoughts unconsciously toward your goals, triggering the power of the universe to help you manifest those goals. I have been amazed by just how much circumstances that come my way resemble the pictures of places and people on my board.

Get a corkboard or pinboard that you can pin things onto (and some pins!) and start choosing the things you would like to display on your board as your prompts to prosperity. Opposite are some suggestions.

* Start cutting out pictures from magazines that remind you of the life you will be living when you are prosperous. The only rule is that they have to feel personal to you and make you feel good. If in doubt, leave them out.

* Get hold of some fake money. There are plenty of board games out there that use quite realistic-looking dollar bills. By the way, it is illegal to photocopy real money in many countries, so stick to the toy stuff. Pick a great wad of paper money and pin it onto your board. It reminds you that there is always enough money to go around.

* Display Chinese money envelopes – the red paper envelopes you see at Chinese New Year, which are traditionally used for gifts of money – up on your board to remind you to attract wealth.

* Chinese symbols of wealth using Chinese characters are also easy to find. Pretty much every Chinese household keeps some sort of symbol up in the home at New Year to remind family members to keep healthy, live long and be prosperous. These symbols make very positive messages to keep on your board.

Looking at your prosperity board

Making a prosperity board is like having a dance of delight with your unconscious every day. Each time you look at it, you will see the person you are going to become one day in the not-too-distant future. It should reflect the key parts of your prosperous life in the years ahead, showing you what you will be doing, being and having.

Every time you look at it, your unconscious begins to believe that this life is a foregone conclusion, which is why it is so important that the pictures and symbols you pick really make your heart sing when you see them!

The great thing about having the Internet is that you no longer need to rely on accidentally finding a picture in a magazine. You can search on the Internet for pictures by subject or keyword. This means that, if you collect enough images, you can even make a slideshow on your computer of your future. You can set this up so that, when the computer goes into rest mode, it starts flicking through your future life. (By the way, you can also take advantage of your computer's sticky-note program if it has one — if you want to pay particular attention to a goal, put it on a 'sticky note' so that it is right in front of you on your start-up screen when you turn on your computer.)

The good thing about collecting lots of pictures quickly is that it prevents your conscious mind from interfering. And your unconscious mind is more important than your conscious mind here because it is your unconscious mind that runs most of your life. It is your unconscious that will provide the thoughts that the Law of Attraction (see page 11) will use to create your future.

Collect a pile or file folder of images and move them around until you feel as if they are in the right place. You will know when it does not feel right. Pin the images to your board or stick them on with glue.

If you are not sure about a picture, please just discard it. Why manifest a future that is almost but not quite right? Why not go for what you really want? Think of your prosperity board as a blueprint for your future. Create a balanced life with activities and quiet times and beauty, as well as pictures of all the things on which you are going to spend your new wealth.

As you put together your board and add bits and pieces to it, feel joy and abundance just in the making of it. Make it large and bright and exciting — just like this wonderful prosperous future you are working toward. Remember that the Law of Attraction works on feelings. The more you can believe that your future is possible and probable, the more of it will be attracted to you. By interacting with the universe in this creative way you are saying: 'I know what I want, and I am relaxed about how I will achieve it.'

Now decide where you are going to hang your board. If you are in a shared home, try to put it somewhere private where it is mainly you who sees it. It is better if you do not get constant comments from other people on what you have chosen. You can put it near a home altar, or in a bedroom or personal study, or check out the prosperity corner of your home from a feng shui point of view and put it there (see page 180). You can even make a mini-collage and carry it with you in a wallet or purse. Key points for your prosperity board:

* Make your future visual: use pictures, not words.

* Choose images that are meaningful to you and make you feel good.

* Keep it private so that you are not influenced by other people's comments.

* Add to your prosperity board whenever you want.

3: Make a prosperity sigil

A sigil is an inscribed or painted symbol or image considered to have special power and is a way of symbolizing your statement of intent. The Law of Attraction responds to the pictures you make in your brain. A sigil is a very powerful symbol of a personal intention that means something only to the person who has made it.

Here's how it works. Suppose that you intend to attract 15,000 for a new car. You write out an intention such as the following:

It is my intention to have fifteen thousand with which I will buy a new car by 30 June.

Notice that although this is a short-term intention (within a year), it is still specific and measurable, and so is something you can focus on with ease. It is also realistic because you have thought about the cost of a new car and why you want it, and your intention has a clear, precise timing associated with it. It is as a result a very believable – possible and plausible – goal.

To make your sigil, you now list all the letters in the statement of intent, then delete any repeated letters.

The statement above reduces to: 'Itsmyneohavfudwcbr30j'

Now you take hold of all your creativity and make a drawing or symbolic interpretation out of this combination of letters. The symbol should be simplified so that you can see the elements within it, and it is

> # A sigil is a very powerful symbol of a personal intention.

also easy to remember.

I sometimes like to make my sigils look like a little cartoon picture of a made-up animal or person. If you anthropomorphize your symbols, you will find that they are very easy to remember. It is entirely up to you and your creativity and imagination.

Next put your energy into the sigil. Sit with the piece of paper in your hands and think about what it symbolizes. See your intention being realized and block out any other thoughts as you do this. You are pouring energy into your intention.

Where to put your sigil

You can now pin the sigil to your prosperity board, or you can burn the paper the sigil is on and thus release attachment to the intention, which symbolizes your trust that your intention will be realised through the Law of Attraction.

Using your sigil as a mantra

Assuming that you have not burned your sigil, you can also use your sigil as a mantra. Chanting a word that has meaning again and again acts as an attraction to the vibration of the intention it symbolizes.

Using your sigil for business

A sigil is such a powerful symbol that you can use it in your business as well. Suppose that you have an intention to create a certain amount of money out of your next sales campaign. In that case, follow the instructions above. Make sure that you have a clear outcome for your campaign. Distil this down into an intention. See the intention in your mind as if it has already happened. Make sure that all your beliefs are lined up to enable this result. If you have any doubts, as always, change the intention or change your beliefs by following the process on pages 20–21.

Next, take the letters of the intention and make a new sigil. Put this sigil on any sales literature going out to your clients. As the literature is dispatched, keep the sigil in your mind's eye as a way of reminding yourself to focus on your intention being manifested. Take action. Ring your clients. Follow up in the usual way. Notice the results.

Feng shui and prosperity

Feng shui is the ancient Chinese art of placement. It teaches how the arrangement of an environment or home can affect the flow of *qi* (*ch'i*), or universal energy, either negatively or positively. By changing the arrangement of objects within your home, you can attract more luck, happiness, love or wealth.

Water

Walk into many Chinese offices and businesses, and you will see a fish tank by the entrance. A fish tank, water plant or water feature or fountain just inside the entrance to your home or bedroom door is seen as a sure-fire way of attracting wealth. Water flowing into a pool symbolizes the flow of wealth accumulating in your life. If you employ a feng shui consultant, he or she will be able to tell you other places in your home where you can put glasses of water to attract wealth. In some systems this varies from year to year and is worked out on the basis of a grid system.

Bells

The sound of bells ringing tells you that good news is on its way. You can buy small metal bells, which you can tie together with red thread or ribbon. Hang these on the door to your home or office, either inside or out, and each time the door is opened it brings in good luck and prosperity.

Chinese coins

Nowadays it is relatively easy to get hold of I Ching coins outside China for feng shui purposes. These are the old-style Chinese coins with a hole in the middle of them. Tie three coins together with a suitable length of red ribbon eight inches long (eight traditionally being considered an auspicious number by the Chinese) and hang the coins inside your front door or put them inside your handbag or perhaps a briefcase you carry with you for business. This traditionally brings you a never-ending flow of income. The reason is that, in Chinese culture, the number three symbolizes the coming together of the energies of heaven, earth and man — in other words, you draw on the creativity of heaven to bring you wealth on earth.

Clutter clearing

In Chinese thinking *qi* — the universal source of energy and giver of life — needs to flow. Clutter in the home blocks the *qi* flow. Where *qi* is blocked it stops the flow of luck into your life. Once you start clearing away the clutter in your home, you will find that you also unclutter your mind.

We often hold on to things we do not really like anymore because we think that we will not be able to afford something new and better. Well, the very act of holding on to the old thing you do not like will ensure that you do not get something better in its place. Think of it like this. You are carrying around in your mind the image of all the things in your home – things you like, things you love, things you do not like. If you think about something you own, you can conjure up its image immediately. It is filed away in your amazing

> ## Where *qi* is blocked it stops the flow of luck into your life.

brain. What do you feel when you think about the things in your home? How many are there because you love them and how many are there just because they always have been there? The old saying is true. A cluttered home really does make a cluttered mind. Why not throw out all the things you do not really love and see how free you feel? It is tremendously liberating. As you think of each item you want to get rid of, think about who you can give it to who will love receiving it.

Give your old things away to a charity, for example, and by liberating these items from your home you free their energy to bring blessings to another home.

The power of using real money

Money is simply a symbol. That wad of cash you have in your wallet or those coins you have in your purse are symbols. Whether it be a dollar, a pound sterling, a euro, a rupee, a yuan or a yen, it is a promise to transfer to the holder a particular amount of value in return for the slip of paper or circle of metal.

Currencies are based on trust. That mix of base metals in the coin is not worth what it says on the outside, nor is that piece of paper in itself worth any more than any other piece of paper, except for the fact that we trust the bank that has issued it to honour its promise to give us certain value in return. The power of this trust makes millions of people throughout the world work hard to get more of these pieces of paper and coins. Each note and coin holds enormous power as a result of all the human energy that goes into it. This makes real money very powerful as a tool for prosperity rituals. True, it is in reality as much a symbol as writing yourself a cheque or using fake game money, but the power of millions of minds forming an energetic connection with this symbol cannot be underestimated.

Take a note from your purse or wallet and look at it. What do you feel as you handle it? What are your associations with it? How willingly would you just give that note away? How much would you like more of these notes or coins?

Using this strong mental and emotional connection we have with cold, hard cash is a great way to learn about our money beliefs and a way to attract prosperity.

Prosperity talismans

One way to harness the energetic power attached to money is to make yourself a talisman. A talisman is an object or piece of jewellery that works as a good-luck charm. A talisman works because of the energy and intent you put into it.

Talismans have been used for many thousands of years for everything from attracting love to warding off evil spirits. Making a talisman using real money provides you with all the emotional and mental associations you need every day to remind your unconscious to focus on creating your intention.

Artwork talisman

This talisman is one you can keep on display in your home or office. Take one or two different paper notes. If you like, you can write your prosperity sigil (see page 178) on the back of each note.

Make a shape out of your note so that it is transformed into a beautiful object that you can look at every day. At home I have two hangings that are made in this way. They look like art, but they are actually made of money and work on the brain as money symbols. If you are not a natural artist, track down an origami book or look up on the Web how to create origami – the Japanese art of paper folding. There are many different shapes you can make with origami, from basic flowers and cranes to more elaborate creations.

If you find you have a particular talent for origami, why not choose to make an animal that represents wealth for you, or perhaps a symbol of what you are going to buy with your wealth? Fold your bill or bills into the appropriate shape. Put your completed talisman somewhere you can see it every day – perhaps the desk from which you work or an area of your home or workspace that is a key part of your day.

Exercise

Prosperity pendants

Why not use a real paper note to make a talisman that you can wear? Again, you can mix rituals and write your sigil (see page 178) on the back of this note if you wish. This will make it even more powerful. There are various ways in which you can do this:

* Take an empty locket and put a real banknote inside it with your prosperity intention or sigil written on the back of the note.

* Take a crystal (see page 184 for crystals particularly associated with prosperity). Wrap the crystal in the paper note and use picture wire or ribbon to bind the money to the crystal.

* Take two pieces of card or similar craft material. Cut them to your desired shape and decorate them in whatever colours and designs you feel drawn to as symbolizing wealth and abundance. Now put the note between the two layers of card and glue them or fix them together. Put a hole in the finished shape and hang it from a necklace or key ring to make a talisman that you can see every day.

Crystals traditionally associated with prosperity

Amethyst

Brings you business success, while at the same time opening you up spiritually, so that you are willing to share your success and abundance with others.

Tiger's-eye or tigereye

Attracts people to you who will help you to build your prosperity, as well as your career, and attracts luck generally.

Carnelian

Helps you to actualize your dreams by taking action.

Citrine

Helps you to acquire and keep wealth.

Jade

Is the stone most associated with wealth in Chinese culture. It is considered very auspicious.

Peridot

Brings money and opportunity.

Red garnet

Is particularly good for bringing abundance to women.

Fluorite

Helps you to use your creativity as a way of creating more wealth and prosperity.

Ruby

Helps you to gain wealth and also protects against its loss.

Topaz

Gets rid of doubts and opens the door of opportunity for you.

Bloodstone

Helps to banish poverty consciousness, so that all kinds of abundance can flow into your life.

Quartz crystals

Are amplifiers of other crystals, prayers and visualizations.

Prosperity bottle

Putting symbols of what you want to attract in a bottle is a very old idea. Find a pretty bottle with a cork. A coloured bottle works well. You could choose a gold or silver one, for example, because of the obvious association with the valuable metals. Purple is also associated with prosperity, so you could paint your bottle in this colour if it appeals. It is important to use a cork that can be taken out as needed, so that you can add things to your bottle.

Wash the bottle and, in your mind's eye, see white light coming down from the highest source in the universe to clean all old energies out of your bottle. Your bottle can contain any sort of charm, scent, herb or crystal that has associations with prosperity. In addition to your choice of charm, add your real money (coins work best in this case), as well as your sigil (see page 178) or statement of your prosperity intentions (see page 153).

Choose an essential oil and plant traditionally associated with prosperity (some examples are given opposite). Add them to your bottle and, when it is ready, cork it up. Light a gold candle to say thank you to the energy of the universe in bringing you prosperity with this symbol you have created.

You can put your prosperity bottle on an altar or by the entrance to your home where you will see it every day. Keep adding coins to your bottle at regular intervals. As you do this, thank the powers in the universe for bringing you prosperity and ask that all the money you give to the bottle comes back multiplied in the form of a flow of wealth into your life. When you do this, it is important to keep the intention that you will play your part in the bargain by putting in the effort into creating the life that you want to live. In return the universe will put in the energy to help you.

Essential oils and plants traditionally associated with prosperity

Essential oils

* Eucalyptus
* Clary sage
* Yarrow
* Patchouli

Plants

* Geranium
* Chamomile
* Basil
* Garlic

Prosperity piggy bank

Your prosperity piggy bank does not have to be shaped like a pig, even though pigs do have positive associations with wealth in some cultures. All you have to do is to choose some kind of jar, bowl or even bag in which to store money.

> ## Working with a group can help to raise the energy of an intention.

The difference with this ritual and the one with the prosperity bottle is that you get to use the money you put inside.

Create a sacred space to carry out the ritual. Find a spot in your home or in your garden where you can light candles and create a place to focus on the ritual. Call in any angels or prosperity deities (see pages 190–197) to help you with the ritual. You can do this by yourself or as a group with friends. Working with a group can help to raise the energy of an intention. To raise the energetic vibration of the space, meditate, play some beautiful music or dance to bring in joyful emotions. As you begin the ritual, this positivity will infect every aspect of it.

Take a banknote out of your purse or wallet. It can be a dollar, pound or any currency you regularly use in real life. Hold it in your hands in this sacred space, and truly appreciate it. It is a means for you to get what you want in your life. Feel it, smell it, notice all the patterns and pictures on the bill.

Now think about what you would like to manifest in your life once you have more of these notes. Be really clear and state your intention out loud. This paper note will become a symbol of your intention. Ask the spiritual helpers present to help you to manifest this intention. If you like, you can add a sigil (see page 178) to the note as well. Place the note in your chosen receptacle. I like to add a separate note for each intention I have — this means that I have put exactly the same energy into each of the intentions, and it reminds me to focus on everything, not just one intention to the exclusion of others.

After you have put the money in the container, ask the universe to begin to multiply the money, so that you are showered with abundance in your life and every intention you have will be realized. Thank the universe in advance for these intentions being realized at some point in the future. Use only the money from the prosperity piggy bank to take steps toward your intentions. For example, if your aim is to save the money to buy a house, use one of the notes to open a bank account. Your intention is that the bank account will be filled with money as this particular note is showered with more and more similar notes.

Use the money from your piggy bank only for things that are directly connected with your prosperity path.

Summary

There are many rituals you can use to boost your prosperity intentions. Choose the ones to which you feel most attuned — those that feel right for you. These are very personal habits. Vary the rituals you use or stick to the one with which you feel the most comfortable.

Why not make a prosperity board, so that you have a visual and emotional link to your goals? Make a prosperity altar and write yourself a cheque for a million pounds or dollars — a promise of your future earnings.

Make sigils to keep around the home or use to boost your business.

Use real money and crystals to create prosperity props — a prosperity bottle, talisman or pendant — or start saving and spending from your prosperity piggy bank.

5: Your Prosperity Helpers

'A wise man should have money in his
head, but not in his heart.'

Jonathan Swift

The invisible spiritual world has many helpers available to us,
whatever our day-to-day needs and concerns.

You may already be familiar with the idea of guides or angels to
whom you can turn for help in times of need. You do not need to
be initiated into a particular religion to call on their help. You
need only to connect with them by desiring them to come into
your life, then ask them for help. The energy of many people
maintains the connection between these highest energies and
our world. The connection is particularly strong because the
thoughts about these deities and helpers are so positive.

In this chapter you will learn about:

* The two Hindu deities who can help you to create
  abundance in your life and undo blocks and obstacles

* The Chinese god of prosperity

* The Celtic bringer of life and her faery children,
  who can help you to create a wonderful life

* A meditation to meet your personal prosperity guide

When millions of people point their thoughts into one idea — in this case a higher being or deity — the power of this spiritual helper grows.

How to choose your prosperity helper

Deities from more than one tradition or religion are described here. You do not have to be religious as such to benefit from building a relationship with them. These are all spiritual helpers who, it is believed, are available to you, no matter what your background is. If you have never before worked with higher energies or guides in any form, take your time to read about these helpers. See what your gut reaction is to working with them. It is important that, whatever you do to help you manifest your goals, you do it with your heart fully engaged. If you are not comfortable with any particular ritual, there is absolutely no point practising it because your inner conflict will produce muddled results.

Be careful not to let either your head or greed override your heart or emotions. Remember that the Law of Attraction does work on thoughts, but always in conjunction with feelings. If you do one thing while you feel another, your feelings will produce the end result.

If you are drawn to a particular deity or guide, talk to them regularly, read up about them, keep pictures of them, celebrate their festival days and think of them as a spiritual parent, or protector or friend. They are always willing to open up a relationship with you.

What can you expect to happen?

These helpers are spiritual beings, which means that they can communicate with you and help you in more than one way. They may alert you to any blocks that are preventing you from manifesting prosperity. They may open up opportunities for you to take action and in so doing manifest your goals.

How do they communicate?

These energetic beings have the power to put people or circumstances on our path that can help us. They may also communicate at night through dreams or during the day by showing us an image or giving us a word message within a meditation. If you use Tarot cards or any kind of divination tool, the helpers will bring you the messages you need through these.

You may also receive clues in your environment. For example, imagine you are trying to make up your mind about whether to take a job that may or may not bring you wealth. You ask your chosen spiritual helper for advice. As you venture out into town to buy your groceries, you see a billboard right in front of you. It says, 'Go for it!' in large letters. Is this a message for you? You are not sure. You pass a store selling sporting goods. You see the same message on a poster. The slogan may be for a well-known manufacturer, but you are noticing it strongly because the universe is communicating with you.

1: The goddess Lakshmi

The goddess Lakshmi is the household goddess of most Hindu families, and so is worshipped by millions of people around the globe. The word 'Lakshmi' comes from a Sanskrit word meaning 'goal', and she is the goddess of wealth and prosperity — not only material wealth and prosperity, but also spiritual. She is worshipped daily and also has the month of October dedicated to her. If you think about it, this means that each day millions of people are pouring their energy and belief into her, making her a very powerful helper for

Lakshmi is one of the oldest goddesses. She was certainly worshipped as long as six thousand years ago, although originally, she may have been an earth mother deity, before being brought into the Hindu group of gods and goddesses. In mythology, she is the wife of Lord Vishnu, the Hindu sun god. It was said that she came out of the churning ocean bringing gifts and was so beautiful that all the gods wanted her.

In pictures, you will see Lakshmi depicted as a beautiful woman with four arms and four hands. She stands or sits on a lotus, and also holds a lotus bud — the symbol of beauty and purity. Gold coins flow from her hands. She wears gold and red clothing. Gold is an indicator of prosperity and red is a symbol of activity. In mythology the wealth Lakshmi brings supports creation. It is an interesting image because it promises a flow of abundant wealth and, at the same time, the lotus

Lakshmi is the goddess of wealth and prosperity.

Lakshmi stands on symbolizes the idea that there is more than just material wealth to aim for in the world. In other words, it is good to create wealth, but not at the expense of other parts of life. She can also help you to find a meaningful career and fulfilment as a means to creating wealth.

Sometimes there are two elephants standing next to the goddess Lakshmi.

Elephants represent the idea of gaining fame or a name because of wealth. They are present in the image to remind us that you should not go after wealth simply to gain a name or fame for yourself, but so that you can share it around and do good things in the world. In other words, prosperity should bring joy to you and all around you.

The good thing about Lakshmi is that she is available as a spiritual energy helper to everyone, regardless of your belief system. If you ask her for help, she will bring you help, especially if you are in dire financial need.

Asking Lakshmi for help

First of all, you need to create your personal connection and relationship with Lakshmi. Start reading about her, her mythology, her character and the help she can give. There are many sources online and in books because she is such a popular goddess, and even in the most orthodox thinking she is open to helping all of us.

Your personal prosperity shrine

If you want to create a devotional relationship with Lakshmi, you can create a little shrine to her. Put her image on your altar, if you like. Make sure that you clean the image by bringing light down from the universe (see page 168) and imagine it taking away any energy that does not belong to the image.

When you ask for energy from the universe in one form, it is good to give it back in another. You can make an offering to Lakshmi in return for the help she gives you. She likes offerings of sandalwood incense, fruit, flowers, money, milk, shells, candles, yogurt, sweets and candies, or sweet things.

If you offer Lakshmi money, it can either be real currency that you put on your altar or fake paper money to symbolize the real thing. She is also associated with the colours red, gold, white and green, so you can also give her offerings in any of these colours.

Place her offerings around her image on the altar.

The Shri Yantra

It is also a good idea to get hold of a picture of the Shri Yantra. You do not necessarily have to go out to buy a copy of this nowadays because there are plenty of images available on the internet.

The Shri Yantra is a symbol of the goddess Lakshmi and also the union of divine feminine and divine masculine, or non-duality. It is a powerful symbol of devotion that teaches concentration of the mind. It is not specifically used for wealth manifesting, but regular meditation with the Shri Yantra can help you focus and gain inner power. It is composed of nine interlocking triangles, which in turn form 43 smaller triangles. The Yantra shows the point between the universe of matter and the universe of spirit or creation, the route through which everything moves from an idea to manifest in reality. You can bring the goddess energy into the Yantra through your offerings and mantras. Notes to keep in mind:

* By feeling gratitude before you receive, you show your faith that the prosperity you seek will cross that dividing point shown on the Shri Yantra. It moves from being an idea in the unmanifest universe to a reality in this world of matter. Ask that whatever is given to you be to your highest good and also to the good and happiness of all. Health, wealth, joy to all.

* Prosperity is a flow. As you receive the blessings of wealth from Lakshmi, give to others. Lakshmi does not like greedy people. She likes you to give to others and share your good fortune.

* Both remain respectful of the goddess and have fun with her. Your relationship with her is a devotional one; at the same time, the spirit world likes light energies such as joy and laughter. Honour Lakshmi by making regular offerings to her shrine and also through devotions during the times of her special festivals, including the full moon.

Active ritual to bring in the goddess

Using a mantra to call or 'invoke' Lakshmi draws her energy near to you. There are many different ones. I like the mantra below:

Om Shring Hring Kling Tribhuvan Mahalakshmyai Asmaakam Daaridray Naashay Prachur Dhan Dehi Dehi Kling Hring Shring Om

Traditionally this mantra is chanted 108 times to bring in the energy most powerfully. If you have never chanted in another language before, this is something you may wish to practise gradually.

As you ask the goddess to come near, you may feel the energy around you change. As soon as you feel her presence, ask for her help. Remember that she will always want to help you because that is her energy and purpose. You can also use sound to bring up the energies. I have a pair of Tibetan bells that I ring to raise energy. You could also use recordings of chants to Lakshmi, which you can play as you think about bringing Lakshmi into your shrine.

When you feel the shift in energies, spend some time meditating with her. Sit quietly and communicate with her about what you want and why. Explain to her what benefits to your life her blessings of material wealth will bring to you.

You can call on Lakshmi at any time. As you call on her, imagine that your wishes have already been granted by her divine power.

Feel gratitude toward Lakshmi with the prayer of thanks, *Om Nameh Lakshmi Nameh* or the prayer of peace *Om Shanti Shiva Shakti*, for granting these wishes.

2: The god Ganesh

Although Lakshmi is the main goddess, I ask for help on prosperity matters, I also make appeals to the Hindu god Ganesh, who helps to remove obstacles around abundance. Ganesh is the elephant-headed deity and the god of wisdom, abundance and prosperity. In mythology he is the child of Shiva, the supreme being. He was born with an ample body that is said to hold within it all the matter of the universe. Vishnu, the Hindu god of love, gave Ganesh his elephant head. He is a happy, loving,

sweet and protective god. His birthday is celebrated sometime in August or September, according to the lunar calendar.

You can ask Ganesh for help with any fear or obstacle you encounter. He is also the god able to grant success. His energy is linked to the movement of energy up and down the chakras (see page 43) and the intellectual mind. This energy makes him very able to help us with everyday concerns.

In some depictions of Ganesh, he holds a bowl of sweet treats in one hand and a noose and goad (a long stick with a pointed end) in another. He uses the goad to push obstacles away from you. He has four arms, which symbolize the vast power he has at his disposal to help you. If you set off down the wrong path, Ganesh will put up obstacles to stop you from proceeding.

Asking Ganesh for help

Form your relationship with Ganesh by reading everything you can about him and getting hold of an image or picture of Ganesh that you can keep on your altar. He likes to receive sweet things as offerings, especially chocolate. You can also give him flowers and incense.

To bring in the energy of Ganesh, stand in front of your altar if you are in your home. Otherwise bring his image into your mind. Call his name.

Now talk to him. He will not answer in words, but he will start to bring events and people into your life to help you with whatever obstacles you are encountering. Tell him your worries and the questions you have, and he will brush aside the obstacles with his goad and open up new opportunities for abundance.

The name Ganesh is very powerful. The most frequently used prosperity mantra linked to Ganesh is: *Om Shri Ganeshaya Namah*

Say it every day, and see what changes come into your life in relation to money and prosperity.

Mantras are not ordinary words. Their sounds link you energetically to the higher vibrations of the spiritual universe. If you are experiencing real blocks when it comes to money, chant the mantra above more than once a day – in the morning and at night. At the same time, visualize money and your prosperity intentions manifesting in your life on this earth plane.

3: Lu Xing, the Chinese god of prosperity

There are three gods generally found together in Chinese images and statues: Fu Xing, the god of happiness, Lu Xing, the god of prosperity, and Shou Xing, the god of longevity. *Xing* is the Chinese

word for 'star' and is sometimes written as *Hsing*. If you have happiness, prosperity and longevity, you will have a very good life in Chinese thinking, so these gods work together and are often referred to simply as Fu Lu Shou. You will find them in folk temples in China and throughout Southeast Asia. They will sometimes be represented by statues, and sometimes the Chinese characters for the three gods will appear on banners near the main temple altar. Lu Xing is sometimes shown riding a stag – an animal that can leap up and over mountainous obstacles. He is also drawn holding a sceptre of power.

Lu Xing is particularly helpful to you if you want a promotion, or a salary rise.

If you are seeking to earn more wealth through your business or by advancing your career, ask Lu Xing for help when you are looking for work as well. He will bring you prosperity, but only if you work hard and help yourself first. His energy is linked to being industrious.

Asking Lu Xing for help

Nowadays it is very easy to get hold of little statues of the three gods Fu Lu Shou from Chinese specialty stores outside Asia. Place the three gods on your altar or have an image of the Chinese characters on your prosperity board (see page 176). In

Chinese businesses and homes, these statues are often placed, according to feng shui guidelines, by the entrance to the home or office to attract good luck into the building and the owner's life. Do not separate the gods from one another, but instead give thanks to all three for the benefits they bring into your life. If you have a particular issue, you want Lu Xing to help you with, hold his image in your mind and ask him to bring you help.

4: Danu, the Celtic creator goddess

Danu (also known as Don, Anu or Dana) is the Celtic creator goddess. The river Danube is named after her. Danu is the mother goddess and as such is a goddess of fertility and abundance, as well as protection. She was also known as Brigantia in the Celtic religion of Late Antiquity, and her legend has evolved in Irish legend to link with that of Saint Bride, or Saint Brighid, in Christianity.

Danu's original worshippers were the Tuatha Dé Danann, the children of Danu, whom it is said retreated to the hills of Ireland, where they became the immortal 'faerie folk'. She is therefore considered the protector of faeries. It is said that the Tuatha Dé Danann were originally alchemists – those who were able to change base metals to gold.

Danu has a very strong feminine energy, so you may be particularly drawn to her if you are a woman; however, there is a balance in all energies and therefore Danu also contains masculine power. As the mother goddess, she is immensely powerful.

Asking Danu and the Tuatha De Danann for help

As well as for helping create abundance in your life, Danu can be called upon for help on matters of fertility and self-esteem. If you have issues about deserving prosperity, then she is the right goddess for you to tune into to help you to overcome any blocking or lack beliefs (see pages 14).

Danu is associated with the faery kingdom, especially Irish faeries or leprechauns, so you can call on their help through her. Some traditions say that there are elementals, or faeries, all around us.

While many of us are used to asking deities or angels for help, belief in faeries is less widespread nowadays. In magical traditions, faeries are said to exist in the invisible planes and so cannot be seen unless you have second sight. Some sensitive people may not see faeries, but they can nevertheless sense their presence because faeries will move objects around the home.

If this view of the spirit world resonates with you, develop a relationship with not only Danu, but also the faeries, and ask them to help you to find prosperity. Leprechauns in mythology have great wealth, which they hide away at the end of the rainbow. Ask Danu to bring you wealth as she brought it to her faery children. Imagine an abundance of wealth flowing toward you. Feel what it feels like as this wealth enhances your life in every way.

If you would like to work with the faeries, you must remember they are said to be as mischievous as depicted in fairy tales. They are also wary of human beings. As children of Mother Earth, they need to know that you care about the earth if you are to make friends with them. Keep plants in your home, cultivate and tend your garden and be kind to the animals and birds around your home.

Find a quiet spot to meditate in your garden. You can even dedicate a spot to the faeries. If you do not have a garden, find a quiet place of nature. As you relax, tell the faeries that you would like to communicate with them, and see what thoughts come into your mind. Start to forge a connection with them, but always remain aware that they have a dark side and can play tricks on unsuspecting humans. Connection with the faeries is not as elevated an energetic connection as you will have with a deity.

I suggest that you also get hold of some faery cards and ask to link into their energy. You can ask the cards to bring you answers relating to any questions you have concerning your prosperity intentions or any blocks or inner issues that have manifested. Just hold the cards in your hand and ask the question. Imagine that Danu is with you as protector of the faeries, so that they know that they must help you. Now pick a card from the pack. The principle is just the same as using a Tarot deck.

Remember that every inner issue preventing you from having immediate wealth can be transmuted into something positive — just as the alchemists are said to have transmuted base metals into gold. The faeries will show you how.

Faery cards can get a little frisky — just like the faeries themselves. I have found that when I handle a deck a card often jumps out of the pack. If this happens to you, pick another card as well but pay particular attention to the card that has jumped out at you. It is always fascinating to see what answer it brings. You can interpret the picture yourself or use the pack's guide.

Making your own faery card pack

If you cannot find any faery cards that you like, you can make your own. This is done by a process of tuning into your intuition and working totally creatively.

* **Step 1:** Get hold of some index cards or plain cards, and some coloured pens.

* **Step 2:** Close your eyes and take a few big, deep breaths to relax yourself. Next, imagine yourself in a quiet place in nature. If you have already designated a part of your garden as a faery meeting place, choose to be there in your mind's eye.

* **Step 3:** Now, still with your eyes closed, imagine the light of the universe coming in and opening up your third eye. This is the point between your eyebrows through which you can have second sight or the ability to see beyond the normal five senses.

* **Step 4:** In your mind, and keeping your eyes closed, I look around this place of nature. Ask that any faeries present give you a glimpse of their shape and form, in a way that is easy and pleasant for you to view them. You may or may not see them at this point.

* **Step 5:** Now open your eyes. Taking a pen in your hand, begin to draw a picture of a faery on a piece of card. Whether it is coming directly from your meditation or even if you think it is just coming out of your imagination, let the drawing flow onto the paper.

You can draw one or more pictures at a session. Draw until the creative urge runs out. To finish each session, in your mind's eye, close up your third eye. Imagine it like an open lotus. To open it, you open up the petals, so that you can see the whole flower. To close it, you fold the petals back in, so that they form a tight, furled bud.

If you repeat this process over days, weeks or months, you will end up with your own 'inspired' pack of faery cards. Each time you use them, they will give you a very personal message because your emotions and vibration will be so linked with them.

Ask the pack a question and pick a card. To interpret the message, let images and words float down into your mind. An idea will spontaneously come to you. If the message is not clear, place the card by your bedside. Ask the faeries to help you to dream the answer to your question. When you awake, take note of the thoughts that have come into your mind.

Exercise

Meditation to meet your personal spiritual guide

As well as gods and goddesses, a personal guide will also be present in the spiritual world who can help you with any issues you have concerning prosperity. This may or may not be the same guide who is there to help you with other areas of your life.

Get to know your guide as you begin your prosperity manifestation because this will help you to maintain a strong link with the spirit world, as well as helping you with any changes you need to make in your attitude towards prosperity.

* Sit or lie down in a quiet place where you will not be disturbed.

* Close your eyes and make sure that you are comfortable. In your mind's eye, open up each of your chakras from the bottom up (see page 43). See the petals of each chakra opening up to show the beauty of the flower and receive the energy of the universe.

* Now take three deep breaths in through your nose and out through your mouth. As you exhale feel the breath relax every muscle of your body.

* Feel your legs and arms relax, then your fingers and toes, then in turn your neck and head. You are now ready to be guided into meeting your personal spiritual guide.

* See in front of you a path. All around you there is natural beauty and greenery. As you walk down this path, let your senses take in the beauty of this green and pleasant place. Notice the grass and the flowers and the trees. Notice the birds singing in the distance. Notice whether there are any tiny clouds in the sky. Feel the ground under your feet. Feel the sun shining on you as you walk. The sun lights the path ahead of you.

* Soon you come to a beautiful little bubbling brook. You see a little wooden bridge. Walk over it, and you will find that the path takes you to a pyramid. The sides of the pyramid are made of clear crystal.

* Enter the pyramid and sit down. There are two seats next to each other. Sit in one of them, and ask your guide to join you in the other seat. You may feel or see your guide entering. Your guide may come in a human-looking form. You may see the whole of the guide or just have a flash of his or her feet or face, or some other part of his or her body. If you are not experiencing any contact, gently look up at the point between your eyebrows (your third eye) to activate your second sight.

* Introduce yourself to your guide, and see whether he or she introduces himself or herself to you.

* As you sit quietly next to your guide, this is your opportunity to ask your guide any questions you have about blocks or intentions. You can ask the best way to make changes in your life or ask questions relating to life purpose or any of your manifestation intentions.

* When your guide answers you, he or she may do so by letting ideas or images come into your mind or he or she may give you a gift. If you are handed a gift, accept it gratefully.

* Continue to have a conversation with your guide. When your guide leaves, exit through the door of the pyramid and walk back down the path. Come back to the present by gently opening your eyes. Take a deep breath and feel the ground beneath you. Make sure that you feel fully present in the room before you move.

* If you have received a gift, think quietly about the meaning of the gift. If you have received an image, think quietly about the meaning of the image.

* In your mind's eye, close up each of your chakras from the top down. See the petals of each chakra closing up into a tight, furled bud.

* To finish and ground yourself, see roots running down from each of your feet deep into the ground.

Using a pendulum

A pendulum is a really simple tool to use. You can use it either to get in touch with your instinct or as a tool to communicate with your spiritual guide. If you do use the pendulum, it is important that you do it from a neutral mindset, because it is easy to influence.

Choose your pendulum carefully. I like to use a metal or crystal pendulum. If you use a crystal one, use one made of quartz not glass and make sure that you clean it with water and salt to remove other people's energies from it.

Hold the pendulum in your hand and ask it to give you a yes. It will either swing horizontally or swing around and around. Ask your pendulum to give you a no. It should give you a different signal. The more you use your pendulum, the better attuned you will be.

To use your pendulum to communicate with your personal guide, start with the intention that you are setting up this relationship.

Hold your pendulum and ask if your guide is present. It should give you a yes. If it does not, work through the guide meditation (see page 198) before trying again.

Now ask if your guide is willing to communicate with you through the pendulum. If you get a clear yes, you can proceed.

Have a question ready to ask your guide. Start with something simple at first, so that you build the relationship step by step and really get to know your guide. Remember that the pendulum can only give yes or no answers. Please be careful, too, not to anticipate what the answer will be, so that you do not influence the pendulum.

As you use the pendulum regularly, you may feel the presence of your guide energetically coming into the room or space you are in. This might be felt as a temperature change or perhaps a tingling in your

> A pendulum is a simple tool to either get in touch with your instinct or to communicate with your spiritual guide.

arm or neck as the guide makes an energetic connection to your auric body. This is the shadow energy body that surrounds you.

If you do not feel anything, that is fine. It does not mean that the guide is not present, but just that you do not tune into energetic changes in that particular way. Store your pendulum in a special box somewhere or even on your altar, where the energies can be kept clean. Please also clean it regularly with water and salt or using any other form of energetic cleaning you may know, so that it can easily receive the higher vibrations of your guide.

Summary

Work with spiritual helpers, including gods and goddesses, to help you to realize your prosperity intentions. Remember to choose who you want to work with because you are genuinely drawn to their energies. Use your heart, not your head.

Do take the time to make a connection with your own spiritual guide for development. Your guide is always there to help you if you ask, but by forging a strong connection through visualization (see page 198) or the pendulum (see page 201) you will open yourself to receive their messages much more easily.

Developing these relationships will help you to know what to do in times when the path ahead is not clear; you will always have a friend and protector on your side who wants to achieve the best for you in your life.

6: Daydream Your Future

'Do not value money for any more nor
any less than its' worth; it is a good
servant, but a bad master.'

Alexandre Dumas

You can boost your visualization power through regular
'daydreaming', and this chapter will show you how. Any kind of
life change can be sped up by practice on the inner levels of the
mind.

Daily or regular practice will help you really get to know yourself
on every level and also create a clearer channel for
communication with the spirit world. You can use any of these
visualizations alongside your chosen prosperity rituals.

In this chapter you will learn about:

* Finding inner space
* Boosting your power of visualization
* Exploring your inner self

Every religious and spiritual practice on the planet teaches some form of meditation or visualization. Monks, priests, nuns, shamans and wise men and women sit quietly or meditate to drumming or music, in order to

> When the conscious mind is stilled, the voice of inner wisdom from the spirit world can be heard more clearly.

still the conscious mind. When the conscious mind is stilled, the voice of inner wisdom that comes from the spirit world can be heard more clearly. This chapter will teach you ways of accessing the wisdom of your inner self and spirit. These methods are all visualizations or 'active' meditations.

Quietening the mind

Here is an easy way to begin. You can either sit in a quiet space where you will not be disturbed or put on some calming classical music in the background to change the vibration of your space. Be careful to choose music that does not have words because the words may interfere with the imagery in your mind. You

do not need to use the same music each time you meditate. Vary it according to what you feel is right on the day. Different pieces will spark off different images in the mind.

This is a very simple relaxation method. All the other daydreaming methods in this chapter follow from this ability simply to sit, breathe and immediately still the mind. As you become more practised, you will no longer need to use the metaphor of the elevator or the room. Instead, simply close your eyes and go down into this quiet place.

When you relax in this way, your mind goes into 'alpha state': your brainwaves slow down and you are able to access the deeper levels of your unconscious mind. Time passes at a different rate in alpha state so, if you find it easy to drift off, remind yourself before you go into this meditative trance that you will wake up at the signal of the piece of music you have chosen (or another pre-set signal).

Simple relaxation technique

Sit comfortably with a straight back in an upright chair. Your legs should be uncrossed. This is the ideal position for meditation because it opens up the energy channel of the spine, which can act as a conductor, bringing down higher vibration energies from the spirit world into this world. Close your eyes and take a big, deep breath in through the nose and out through the mouth. Let your body relax. Let your arms rest gently on your lap, and let your legs sink into the floor.

Now take two more deep breaths, once again inhaling through the nose and exhaling through the mouth. As you breathe out, feel any tension just drop out of your body. Say to yourself: 'As I breathe out, all tensions and worries and stresses of the day melt away into the floor below. I am deeply relaxed.'

Feel your eyelids become heavy. If you wish, you can check your eyelids: slowly open them and close them, feeling the relief of being able to close them again and go deeper into sleep – this wonderful state of daytime dreaming meditation.

Now imagine that there is an elevator in front of you. You walk into the elevator and see that there are ten floors. You are currently on the tenth floor. Press the button with '1' on it, so that you can go all the way down. As the elevator descends, each button lights up in turn. You see the numbers flashing in descending order: 10, 9, 8, 7, 6, 5, 4, 3, 2, 1.

When you reach the first (ground) floor, you will see the door to a room in front of you. This is your room of relaxation. There is a bed here. It looks so comfortable.

Enter the room, lie down and relax completely.

Remain in this place for five minutes or so at first (or 15 minutes or more if you want to extend the time as you become more practised).

When you want to come out, just get back into the elevator and press the button to the tenth floor. See the numbers going up from one to ten. When you reach the ninth floor, feel the energy beginning to return to your body. As you reach the tenth floor, take a big, deep breath. Open up your eyes, and slowly bring yourself up to conscious awareness, feeling the energy return to your legs and arms, eyes and mouth, head and neck. Feel your breathing come back to normal. Wake up easily, and when you are ready and feel grounded you can get up.

> Different pieces of music will spark off different images in your mind during meditation.

Boosting your visualization power

Visualizations are guided or self-guided methods of imagination and daydreaming. When you visualize, you are asked to see ideas or symbols as you relax. You may also spontaneously become aware of symbols that the inner self and spirit send you as messages. These symbols may not mean anything to you in the moment of meditation; however, after you complete the meditation, you can think about their meanings.

Symbols and their meanings will either be very personal to you — for example, a dog reminds you of the dog you used to own when you were a child and the feelings you had then — or archetypal (a meaning that is common to everyone) — for example, a rose symbolizes love.

How do I know that I can visualize

It is important to say at this point that we can all visualize, although sometimes people will say that they cannot do it. If you think that you might be one of those people, consider this question: What does your bedroom look like? Did you get a picture? See, you can visualize.

OK, here's another question to show you that you can not only visualize what is currently in your present, but also what does not yet exist. Go back to that picture that just appeared in your mind and change it. Now imagine getting a big paintbrush. There are three big paint pots in front if you, each in a different colour: red and yellow and green. Imagine dipping the paintbrush into one of those pots of a particular colour and splashing it all over the walls of your bedroom. Now what does that look like? Did you have a picture? If the answer is yes, you can definitely visualize.

Visualization does not just take place within one sense.

Another important thing to remember is that visualization does not just take place within one sense. When you get a visual picture, you can also engage your other senses — touch, taste, smell (and even hearing, in the sense of imagining particularly evocative sounds). The more you do this when you visualize your dreams coming true, the more you will boost the power with which they do so.

Again, it is simple to demonstrate how well you do this already. Close your eyes and imagine that you are holding a lemon in your hand. Bring the lemon up to your lips and take a big bite out of it. Can you imagine the taste of the lemon?

Most of us when we do this screw our faces up a little or feel our mouths going dry because the mind reacts so quickly to the idea of the distinctive acidic taste of the lemon.

How about this? What would it be like if you walked into your kitchen or a restaurant that you know well and you smelled bread baking? Or there was coffee on the stove? How strong were those images for you?

Does your image need a boost when it comes to your sense of smell? Imagine something with a really disgusting smell. How did your body react simply to the words on the page? Did you tense slightly or wrinkle your nose? Then the image is working. Well done.

Next, to touch. What does it feel like to be snuggled up in bed, wrapped up warmly? Did you get a picture with a feeling when you read this question?

What does it feel like to have the sun beating down on you, so that you feel warm all over, bathed in its rays? What does a favourite piece of clothing feel like when you think about it? What does it feel like to hold someone close: a lover, or baby

> Your intention for a visualization is key to the success, because thought affects everything we do.

or a pet? What does it feel like to be held in someone else's arms?

How about your feelings? Think very quickly of a time when you felt mildly stressed or uncomfortable in a situation. How quickly do you experience the same feeling? Notice what your body does in response to the image. When we are stressed or feeling any kind of negative emotion, we shrink inward — both on a physical and an auric level.

Now, to feel good again as quickly as possible, think about these situations. Imagine being with a group of people and really finding something funny — you might be listening to a story or joke or watching a show or film. Can you imagine being with someone and being really happy? Can you imagine doing something and feeling very excited?

When you think of any of these situations, notice how quickly your body recovers — which means your vibration lifts very quickly as well. Notice how quickly you can adjust your thoughts — in a matter of seconds. Notice also how easy it was to visualize with feelings attached — which is very important for working with the Law of Attraction (see page 11).

The importance of intention

Your intention for a visualization is key to the success of your visualization because thought affects everything we do. As with every ritual, be clear ahead of any visualization why you are doing it and what outcome you want as a result of doing it.

If you have several different cosmic orders such as a new car, home, new refrigerator etc., you can either visualize yourself having these during one daydream, or you can set up different rituals that relate to the different intentions. Make sure you are clear for each goal why you want it. What you really want on a conscious and unconscious level will be what is manifested.

What can you expect to happen as a result of meditation?

Even though it may seem that you are not doing a great deal by sitting and imagining within your mind, this inner work has immediate effects on your outer reality. This works in a similar way to carrying out any regular ritual such as the ones described in previous chapters. Even if you do not think you have experienced a great deal within the visualization, if your intention is clear, you will still see results.

After doing this inner work for a while, you will find clues in your everyday life that your circumstances are changing. You may be offered work or another opportunity to earn or invest money. Or you may spot an

opportunity to make a connection that leads you toward one of your prosperity goals.

If, on the other hand, your intentions when you do these

If your intention is clear, you will see results.

visualizations are unclear, you will get unclear results in your life, and it is easy to go off your path again. It is really worth spending a few minutes thinking about the major goals that you want to manifest and the changes you want to make ahead of each visualization.

Exercise

Smash through your prosperity blocks

* Relax by breathing deeply and stilling the mind. Do this technique with or without music. You can use the elevator technique (see pages 204–205) or simply relax by closing your eyes and relaxing your muscles. Breathe deeply to release all the tension.

* Enter your relaxation room. As you do this, you notice that there is a door that opens outward. Walk through it.

* Imagine that you are now standing in a garden. Look around the garden, and notice what state it is in. Is the garden already in full bloom or are the seeds yet to blossom? Perhaps there is some weeding needed or it may already be perfectly ordered.

* Spend five minutes here in the garden noticing what you experience as you explore. This is the garden of your unconscious mind. When you spend time in it, you will get to know yourself better. Enjoy the experience of being here.

* Now, ahead of you, notice there is a path. Walk along the path until you come to a block of some kind. It may appear in the form of a wall or an object. You cannot move around this block until you get rid of it.

* Notice on the ground or next to the path that there is an object you can use to smash through the barrier. You can grow to whatever size or strength is needed to wield this tool and smash through the barrier, so that it is totally removed from the path. This barrier is a prosperity block.

＊

* Once you smash through the barrier, you will see in front of you that the path leads to a body of water. There is a waterfall and a box of treasure within it, symbolizing the flow of prosperity in the universe and the treasure you will take from it. Step into the waterfall and feel yourself showered with the abundance of the universe. Take whatever treasure you like from the box. Imagine that there is so much you can have whatever you want and bring it back with you along the path into the garden.

* Before you leave the garden, thank the universe for the abundance that it is giving to you now and in the future.

* Walk back into your room and out through the normal door. If you are using the elevator technique, press the buttons to bring yourself up.

* Bring yourself back into conscious awareness by taking a few deep breaths to bring yourself up out of this light trance. Next, open your eyes and come back into the room, feeling happy, rich and prosperous, and filled with gratitude for all you have received.

You can repeat this meditation whenever you like. You may well find that your garden changes, giving clues to your state of mind at any one time. Do take note of what you find: whatever it is will be absolutely perfect for where you are right now. Pay attention to the feelings you get when you are in the garden. Your spirit guide will alert you to anything you need to know through feelings, as well as through messages. If you like, adapt the guided visualization in Chapter 6, asking to meet your guide in the garden as a way of receiving messages here.

Goal booster

To boost your visualization power, use the relaxation method earlier in this chapter to quiet your mind (see pages 204–205). Do this exercise with or without music. Before you begin, decide which of your goals you are going to visualize within the meditation. Again, if it helps, you can enter your relaxation room and take a different door into this new place described below. If you are more practised, simply relax and find yourself immediately in the corridor.

* **Step 1:** Imagine that you are walking down a corridor with one or more doors. This is the corridor to your future. As you walk down the passage, feel how excited you are about the fact that you are about to view this future life. As you come to the right door, open the door handle and walk through into your new life.

* **Step 2:** Now explore every aspect of this new life in as much detail as possible. If you want to change any of it, you can do so by manipulating the pictures. For example, supposing your intention is to manifest the money you need to open a clothing boutique. Imagine that the door takes you straight into the boutique. Walk around the space and notice what it looks like – as if you are a building inspector coming to check that the builders and decorators are doing a good job. You have the power to order anything in here to be changed. Go into every corner. Lift up the products you are selling; smell, examine and feel. If you want to change the wall colour, change it. If you want to expand the size of the retail space, do so.

Notice your appearance in the future. Notice what you are feeling. If you want to change anything in your picture, then do it. You can do it in an instant. When you are satisfied with what you see and the way you feel about it, leave the room and shut the door, knowing that everything is in place.

Sometimes, as you do this exercise, your spirit guide will give you a message linked with this future

> Be alert for messages which may appear in the form of an image or idea coming into your mind.

about an opportunity that you need to seize or a step you could take to bring it closer to you. Be alert for messages. These may appear in the form of an image or idea that suddenly comes into your mind or in a figure who appears in the dream and tells you something.

Sometimes, too, you will notice an object that stands out in the daydream and makes an impression on you that you carry back to your waking consciousness. If this happens, be sure to make a note of it and write down all the associations you have with the object or consult a book on dreams and their images/symbols. There are many archetypal images that we share as human beings that have standard interpretations. Other meanings may be personal to you. You will know when you have hit the right interpretation because it will 'feel' right.

If you get a picture of the dish without the flavour – that is, a picture of your goal without any pleasure or joy attached – change the picture.

Take the time to explore each of your dreams in turn. If you do not find it easy to explore these, do the exercise opposite to improve your visualization. Always pay attention to your thoughts but also to your feelings. It is the strength of feelings attracted to thoughts that the Law of Attraction really responds to.

Banknote visualization

This is a very simple visualization exercise. You do not even need to go into a meditation or trance state to practise it. Simply close your eyes. Being able to see money in detail in your mind's eye makes it easier to visualize having wealth in your life in the future.

* **Step 1:** Hold a banknote in your hand. With your eyes closed, explore in your mind what it looks like. This is a way of stimulating the visual sense. Imagine your hands holding the note. See its colour, its size and any pictures or patterns on it. Sense in your mind what it feels like to hold the note.

* **Step 2:** Once you have a clear picture of the note in your head, you can begin to manipulate your imagined image.

* **Step 3:** Now see yourself in the picture holding the note. Put it into your purse or wallet and imagine walking into a store or shop. Take out your purse or wallet and remove the note. Imagine that you are spending this money in the store. Think about what you are buying with it. Whatever you buy is going to give you great pleasure, so you gain enormous satisfaction from paying for your purchase with the note because you feel happy with what you receive in exchange. Please

give yourself the time to feel the positive emotions fill your body as you hand over the note.

The ever-filling wallet

The next stage of this visualization exercise is to imagine that your wallet or purse is always full. However many notes you take out of it, it always remains stuffed full of more notes.

* **Step 1:** Let's imagine a scenario. Put yourself back into the store or a place where you are going to buy something you really want to have in your life. Perhaps it is a big purchase such as a car, for example. Think about what it is going to be before you close your eyes. By the way, it does not have to be an object; it could be an activity or any purchase that contributes to you discovering a way of life that makes you fulfilled and content. This includes paying bills.

* **Step 2:** Now, quiet your mind and take yourself immediately to the scene. You can see whatever the purchase is that you are going to buy. You feel satisfied that by paying for this your life becomes better and better, and it enables other positive choices in your life. Get clear on this in your mind before you proceed.

* **Step 3:** Imagine that you are at the counter or payment point ready to make your purchase. You can see the person you are about to pay. You take out your wallet or pocketbook. As you open it up, you see that it is filled with banknotes. Take out the notes and spend them in your mind. As you take out the notes and hand them over to the seller, notice that your wallet keeps filling up. No matter how much you take out, the amount of money left in your wallet either remains exactly the same or even multiplies. This is because it is your special ever-filling wallet. It will never empty because it is directly linked to the flow of the universe and so will constantly fill whenever necessary.

* **Step 4:** As you see the picture of yourself doing this, be appreciative of the abundance with which the universe is showering you. Enjoy this feeling of wealth and prosperity. Thank the universe for your ever-filling wallet.

> Being able to see money in detail in your mind's eye makes it easier to visualize having wealth in your life in the future.

Belief booster

This is a guided belief-change meditation that you can use from time to time to help you to really feel the changes that are taking place in your thought processes.

* **Step 1:** Think of a belief that you would like to have. Think about any belief that would lead to a positive boost to your prosperity. If you cannot think of one immediately, write down a belief that you no longer want to have and think about what the opposite belief would be. Think about what kind of opportunities having this belief would attract into your life. Can you imagine how much better your life will be in every way when you adopt this belief?

* **Step 2:** Sit quietly. Close your eyes and take a few deep breaths to still the mind. Let your body relax. Again, you can use the elevator relaxation method and enter your relaxation room (see pages 204–205).

* **Step 3:** Imagine that you are somewhere pleasant and relaxing. This could be outside in nature — on a beach or in a beautiful meadow or wood — or in a beautiful room. In front of you is standing a new you. Look at this new you from a distance.

* **Step 4:** Imagine that, as you watch, you are becoming a very powerful

magician. Give yourself a wand or any other magical tool that will enhance your power. You have the power to endow this new you with wonderful qualities and new empowering beliefs that will make the new you into a natural prosperity magnet. You can use this power now.

* **Step 5:** Think about the new prosperity belief that you would like to have. If there is anything you can add to it at this point that will make it an even more powerful thought, do this now.

* **Step 6:** Take your wand or point your finger or use any other magical tool you have at your disposal. You are going to command that belief to drop as a thought form into the energy of the new you, so that all old thought forms that you no longer want are dispersed forever.

* **Step 7:** See the belief dropping into the body of the new you. As this happens, the energy of the thought will start to change the new you. You may see this as a change in the energy field of the new you, or light flooding in.

* **Step 8:** Next, step into the body of the new you, so that you are one person again. Feel the difference in your body in this space as you and the new you integrate. As this is happening and as you are taking

on this new belief, start to imagine how differently you will behave. You may notice differences immediately in the way you look at the world around you.

* **Step 9:** See yourself leaping into the future to a time far enough ahead that you can become aware of the changes that have taken place as a result of adopting this new belief. Pay attention to what has changed positively. Are you behaving differently? Do you have different things in your life? What kind of person have you become?

* **Step 10:** Once you have fully absorbed the change in your mind, emotions and body, take a few deep breaths. Open your eyes and come back fully to the room.

* **Step 11:** Finally, with your eyes open, think about how much more powerful you are now. Imagine a future situation and how you will react to it. What has changed? What do you think now?

> This guided belief-change meditation can help you to really feel the changes that are taking place in your thought processes.

Energetic visualizations to heal yourself

Practise energetic visualizations to heal any negative beliefs and emotions they produce in relation to prosperity. Carry out the ritual on the next page if you feel any deep negative emotions, including fear, revolving around money.

This technique removes past, negative thought forms from the aura and also helps to stop you from being overly sensitive to group beliefs. If you are a very sensitive, open person, you will pick up other people's beliefs and they will overwhelm your own intuition. On an energetic level this can be seen in the energetic body as thought forms.

You may know that you have an energetic body, as well as a physical body. Within your energetic body there are seven power points known as 'chakras'. These are like battery chargers for the energy body. They need to be kept healthy for your mind, body and spirit to be in balance. (See page 43.)

People who possess 'second sight', the ability to see with the third eye, may be able to see negative thought forms within the energetic bodies that surround our physical bodies. Thought forms look like dark patches or clouds within the clear energy of the outer aura. Negative thought forms are sticky, and they attach themselves to our energy when we have strong emotions or hurts from the past that linger in our present.

If you do not have psychic abilities or second sight, you can still practise this visualization, and it will have an

This energetic visualization removes past, negative thought forms from the aura.

effect on your belief system because energy is linked with thought. You just have to hold the intention that, whether or not you can see thought forms in the way that a psychic person can see them, the outcome will be the same.

Thought-form visualization

The visualization below releases negative or blocking thought forms from the aura. After they have been released, you will feel a sense of lightness, joy, relief or happiness. You can practise this visualization as often as you like.

* **Step 1:** Take at least three deep breaths to quieten your mind. Now visualize your body surrounded by energy. Visualize the seven energy centres, or chakras, within your

body (see page 43). Imagine that they are like flowers with petals that can open or shut.

* **Step 2:** Imagine that your crown chakra (the one at the top of your head) is opening up like the petals of a flower to let in the white light of the universe. This white light is love, and love is the most powerful force in the universe. Let it flow through your body and into all of your chakra energy centres. (Another way to visualize this is a large, white net capturing everything in its path.)

* **Step 3:** At the same time, imagine roots growing out of your feet and going deep into the earth, so that you are grounded with the power of the earth as you go through this process.

* **Step 4:** Now imagine that you have a hose running from your solar plexus (the site of the solar plexus chakra, see page 43) out into the earth. If you find any dark patches in your energy field, visualize the white light pushing them out into the earth. The earth is a natural healer. As the dark patches leave your body, the earth will transform their energy and use it to heal.

* **Step 5:** Once every dark patch of energy has left your body, pull the hose back into your solar plexus and close up the energy centre (chakra) once more. Visualize this

as a flower closing up its petals.

* **Step 6:** Close each of your chakras in turn in your mind's eye, but keep your crown chakra open just a chink so that light can continue to come in. Do the same with your root, or base, chakra. (See page 43).

* **Step 7:** Keep the roots coming out of your feet into the ground in place, so that you stay connected with the world of matter, as well as the world of spirit, every second of every day.

* **Step 8:** To finish the process, imagine the white light swirling around you, forming a protective net that pushes away any negative energies that try to come into contact with it. Next, in your mind's eye, run a silver-grey cord around you, over the top of your head and under your feet. Let it swirl around your body. You now have a protective energetic seal surrounding you.

* Step 9: If you are a very sensitive person who absorbs other people's energies too easily, every morning when you wake you can surround yourself in a white bubble of light. Make sure that the light goes all the way above your head and under your feet, as if you are encased in a big, white bubble bag.

This will prevent you from attracting draining or negative energies.

Summary

You now have the basic building blocks by which you can manifest as a reality any change in your life circumstances that you can imagine. If you are experiencing any particular blocks or want to accelerate the changes, use the techniques in this chapter.

By working on your inner world regularly, you will experience immediate and permanent changes in your outer world. Practise your power to visualize. See how easy it becomes to manipulate the images so that you can create future memories — images of yourself in the future.

Explore your inner garden and make it beautiful and ready to receive the prosperous life that you deserve.

7: Final Words on Prosperity

The methods in Section Two of this book ensure that you have a vision of what you want and the kind of life you want to create. They mean you can start to get rid of any inner or outer blocks that are in the way of achieving it. I hope that you will remember that there is no point going after money alone — you are unlikely to get wealth for wealth's sake. The service you give to get that wealth is as important to creating happiness in your life as what you do with this prosperity.

Be bold in your visions of your future and focus on them. You will not know every step of your journey to achieve prosperity by the time you have finished reading this guide. That's absolutely OK. You do not need to. You are only a co-creator of your future. Yes, you must play your part, but the universe will also play its part by bringing you opportunities as you go along. Remember to stay patient. Most people who build great wealth do it over a lifetime — not all in one go. Your life will improve as you journey, regardless of this.

The abundant garden of the universe

Your job is to plant the seeds and water them — make your intentions and take actions toward them.

It is the universe's job to make the seeds grow under the surface of the soil, providing them with all the nutrients they need to sprout above the surface, then blossom into flower. It is then your job to thank the universe for its efforts on your behalf and to admire the flowers. In this way, you ensure that the next time the universe will produce a whole field of blooms for you.

Keep records of your manifestations

Always keep track of your manifestation work. It is important that you can see the results you get from the effort you have put in. Manifestation can be as easy as simply asking for something and receiving it. It can flow very easily as a result of a small change to your beliefs or just by you putting the time into making a prosperity board (see page 176). When it happens that easily, however, sometimes people can become a little dismissive or complacent, and say things like: 'Oh, but that would have happened anyway,' or 'But that was just a coincidence,' or 'Yes, but that can't have been manifestation because it

was me who made it happen.'

Yes — that's right. It was you. It did seem like a coincidence. It did happen easily. BUT... Would it have happened if you had not set your intention years before? Would it have happened if you had not spent time examining your beliefs and passions?

You do not need to be obsessive about your record keeping but setting aside a nice notebook is a good idea. You can make it into a

> ### Make your intentions and take actions toward them.

specific book for your prosperity manifestations, keeping any other manifestations separately, but that is up to you. On the front of the notebook, draw or attach a picture that reminds you of what you are attracting into your life.

You can also put your prosperity sigil there if you like (see page 178).

Write down in your notebook what you have done to change your thinking, any rituals you are performing and the list of your intentions. Next, note down what you manifested and when. Pay attention to how near it was to your original intention. You may find that there are times when you get everything you ask for and others when manifestation is a little more blocked.

Blocks

There are only a few blocks that can stop your intention manifesting:

* Not giving your vision enough time to happen.
* Not really believing deep down that it can happen.
* Wanting rather than expecting.
* Being muddled, confused or ambivalent about what you really want.
* Not feeling your future can happen.
* Not playing your part.

If you feel that you are blocked, examine both your beliefs and your goals. Make sure that you have paid enough attention to making the changes you need to make. The Law of Attraction functions perfectly. If there is a block there is always something, YOU need to change.

> If you feel that you are blocked, examine both your beliefs and your goals.

Your thoughts

Remember that the thoughts you have — both conscious and unconscious, second by second, even if you are not aware of them — are crucial to what will manifest in your life. If you look at most of the millionaires on the planet, they had long-term visions and, even if they came from very tough backgrounds, they did not remain stuck in that mindset because their beliefs were just so compelling. If you still have not overcome any negative conditioning from the past or present, family or peers, please take the time to undo these beliefs. This is not a one-off process. Sometimes we are alerted to old beliefs only by new life experiences.

Feed your mind with visions of your future and take the time to think about what beliefs would support this vision. If it helps, keep looking around for role models who hold these positive beliefs whom you can observe at close quarters or see in the media.

Your emotions

Pay attention to your emotions. These are clues to your thoughts and especially to unconscious beliefs that you may not have put into words. Be clear that your heart and not your head is leading you when you make your vision, otherwise you will not get a future that you truly want. If you feel bad, something is wrong. You have gone off-track in some way. There may be a fear to be dealt with. You may need to make adjustments to your intentions for your future.

When you get good feelings going, you will know that you are back on track. Feeling good is designed to be your dominant way of being – it is your birth right to be happy. Being happy connects us to the source – or God and the universe.

When you have a clear expectation of receiving your intentions – rather than just wanting or hoping for them –happiness will be your default emotion.

See the opportunities

Make sure that you are picking up on any opportunities and signals that the universe is throwing in your direction to help you to bring your vision to you faster. When you pick up on these signals, act. Remember that our manifestations come about as a result of actions – just like the Fool card in a Tarot deck (see page 13). Jump quickly when you are inspired to act and think afterwards. If you know where you are heading, the route is generally clear. If you are not sure what you want to create, you may miss some of these inspired opportunities. If no

opportunities appear to be coming your way, go back and check that you really know what kind of future you are seeking to manifest.

Remember that the universe is a universe of abundance, so if an opportunity is missed there will be another. The universe will hear the intentions you have set as a future memory and do everything it can to help you realize them. It will bring you opportunity after opportunity for action. This is why, if you have not manifested exactly as you want yet, you must nevertheless remember to thank the universe for whatever you receive. This will keep you in the way of abundance thinking. The universe has followed your instructions as precisely as possible for the moment.

Keep records on a quarterly, half-yearly or yearly basis. Review and reward your successes. Notice the changes you can make to become even more effective. Adjust your prosperity board (see page 176) if need be. Add some rituals to your regular practice. Examine your beliefs and how well you know your own thinking.

Sit and meditate on what you have achieved and not achieved. If you have manifested money but not prosperity, take as much time as you need to really let yourself dream. More often than not, the biggest blocks to manifesting are not knowing what one wants or not setting aside enough time for it to manifest. Being very specific and clear in your 'whats', in terms of ten or twenty years' time, brings in such a pull of energy from you to the universe it often unravels a lot of belief blocks along the way.

Commit to yourself and your unique vision for your future, and you will reach it and live a rich and fulfilled life.

May you realize all your dreams and transform your life. Be happy and prosperous.

Summary

Now that you have reached the end of this section my wish for you is that your story has a happy ending as well. Take all the time you need to change your life and make it how you want it to be. Learn through practice how the Law of Attraction can bring prosperity into your life every day. Remember: The Law of Attraction is perfect. Clear your blocks, visualise as specifically and consistently as you can the future you intend to create. Take action towards it.

Taking steps towards prosperity

* Decide what prosperity means for you personally, recognising that it is always more than just money.

* Change the story of your past to a happy one. Look at the beliefs you hold about yourself, your past, money and your future. Begin to change your lack beliefs to abundance beliefs.

* Start now with a fresh sheet of paper and begin to dream the life you want to create.

* Look to the invisible universe and the helpers who live within it to help you realise your dream of a loving future.

* Rely on the Law of Attraction as a perfect means of bringing the future you choose to create into your life. Recognise that thoughts and the feelings attached to them will bring the future you deserve. If you aren't getting the future you want, change your thoughts and feelings about what you deserve.

* Set your intention to co-create your future and show your commitment to the universe by taking action towards what you want every day.

* Change your relationship with money. Learn to enjoy it. Get rid of any fear you have attached to the idea of money. Money is simply a means to an end. It is the medium through which you can create more good feelings in your life.

* If you still aren't achieving your goals, change the timescale. Let go of the date you attached to your goals or push your date forward. A watched kettle seldom boils. By being over-attached to results, you push the outcome you want further away.

* Allow enough time for your future to manifest.

* Remember that you can't see the workings of the universe any more than you can see a seed beginning to grow under the earth. When you think nothing is happening there may be something going on that you need to pay attention to.

* Then if you still aren't getting what you want, change something. Change what you are thinking, doing or seeking to create.

* Notice if you have a really clear and specific picture of your future.

* Notice if your picture is good for you and all around you. Make sure it brings balance into your life by questioning why you really want this.

* When in doubt take different actions towards your new future and see what happens.

* Use ritual to reinforce your intentions for your life.

* Watch the people and circumstances coming into your life. As your life begins to change one of the first clues is in the people and events you attract.

* Pay attention to your nighttime dreams. If you find it easier, use day-time mediation to seek messages from the spiritual universe.

* Forge a relationship with a spiritual guide and let him or her help you.

When you have done everything then trust. Trust is an abundant thinking pattern. Trust and let go, relying totally on the universe to bring you, if not exactly what you have asked for, definitely a future which is even more to your higher good.